"PARTING NOTES"

A Connection With The Afterlife

A Psychic Medium
Connects to Share
Firsthand Personal
Experiences of
Life After Death

APRIL CRAWFORD

ISBN: 1-4033-0607-9 (e-book)
ISBN: 1-4033-0608-7 (Paperback)
ISBN: 1-4033-0609-5 (Hardcover)

Library of Congress Control Number: 2002102474

This book is printed on acid free paper.

Printed in the United States of America
Bloomington, IN

Notes, Book Design, and Art: Allen Crawford
For information e-mail address: TrChannel@AOL.com
www.PartingNotes.com

1stBooks - rev. 09/23/02

"You do not know us by name. We exist in the peripheral of physical life...

We are all alive and well...All that she is about to reveal to you is true...

Each of these letters will alter one person's life, or perhaps many in unison. After you have read them, share them. That was the intent in which they were written.

Read with love.
All of us."

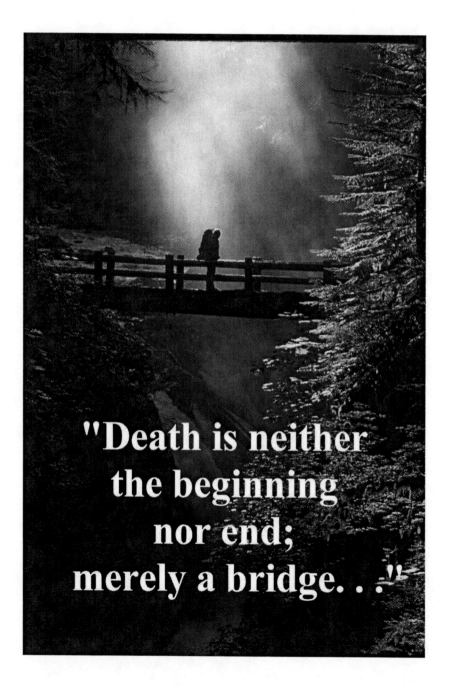

"Death is neither
the beginning
nor end;
merely a bridge. . ."

Contents

Forward By Bubba

In your period of self imposed mourning may we offer you this. Suppose the sun rose in a most pristine fashion. The warmth of the rays fell upon your face with a delicacy that brushed your most inner self with a breath of heaven you had only before imagined. Every nuance of your physical superimposed itself in your eye and could no longer improve upon itself. The body so long clung too beginning its decline. No longer concerned with breath your focus drawn to the crevasse that beckoned you to eternity. You decide in a heartbeat to go ahead and prepare a spot that love would dwell for all those dear to you. The moment grasped, you no longer are concerned with the inhale & exhale of the time line. You become motionless against the pulse. Realizing the pulse is but a musical rhythm, the beat becomes you and you the beat. Stepping forward you go. Not leaving but leading to a new destination that will remove the end point for all you love. Not death, not ending, but beginning.

If you are the first it is difficult to be left behind. We know we seem unfinished and are wrought with fragmented goodbyes but we await you refreshed, and free from physical tragedy we are eternal. So are you.

As much as I wanted to stay the beckoning of the cosmos was an aphrodisiac that opened my essence to my true potential revealing my spot in the fate of those who loved me. I relinquished any selfish desire for the good of the masses rather than the good I foresaw for myself. In doing so the release of my soul shall have impact on the growth of those I have realized I love more than myself. My embrace shall follow you through out your dramas till we meet in harmony, our essences thus more evolved will exist on a plane of love for eternity.

I was not just a friend but a life force. That pulse of life a victory in that I realized my potential. All "lives" should be so prosperous.

Thank you.

Bubs.

[Note: Bubba was, and is, a dear and feisty friend who passed away from an apparent heart attack in the Spring of 2001 after a brief but severe kidney problem that he actually started to recover from under intensive doctor prescribed in-home care (that he did not like). The medium cried intensely when he "died", and she cried again when she read this message for the first time. Even though this message was written to her from the Other Side...from Bubba...using April's own hand...this message came through as a complete surprise and at an extremely emotional time for us both. This time April's tears were tears of joy at the re-connection with her dear friend, confirming that it was *his* choice, that of course he is all right, and that they will indeed meet again. Bubba also insisted that this be the forward to the book!]

Introduction: My Wife Is A Deep Trance Psychic Medium

I first met April Crawford, the author of *"Parting Notes"*, when we were just discovering, much to her chagrin at the time, that she was a natural full trance and full body psychic voice medium.

What this means is that April could and still can effortlessly enter into a very deep dream-like trance state, and you could have a two-way conversation through her *directly* with "dead" people. And lots of them wanted to talk when we first started and the "waiting line" is even longer it seems today.

At first this remarkable ability was somewhat startling to us. We literally had to place pillows all about April to prevent her from hurting herself when after relaxing into a trance state, she would often completely collapse and fall to the floor only to get up in a minute or two, her body now animated and speaking for someone else, sometimes with eyes wide open and sometimes with eyes tightly shut. Some remained seated but many could actually get up and walk around the room. The connection was always clear and there seemed to be no limit, other than our available time, regarding who or how many could talk with us. April could maintain the connection for hours at a time. Afterwards, she always felt great. Today, April still feels refreshed after a session.

In those early days April was concerned that her newly discovered psychic abilities made her "weird or something". Originally April met with a few of our friends some evenings just for the social fun and good conversation. In the beginning she wasn't at all seriously interested in the whole mediumship thing. Before her first remarkable experience April really didn't know if she even believed that mediumship was real. She certainly never expected to find out that she was a full trance medium herself. Little did she know. Little did any of us know.

At April's request her newly discovered psychic mediumship abilities were kept strictly private among our close little group of friends. April and I were married about a year after those first events.

Fast-forward about 10 or so years to present day. April now has pinpoint and elegant control over her mediumship. She is able to enter into trance states so subtly that it can be just the turn of her head and you can be speaking to a spirit. It is fully interactive and just as conversational as talking with friends or family here. It can take place anywhere and at anytime. Upon her return to her body, April rarely remembers anything that was said while she was "out". There is no ceremony necessary for April to do this, although a glass of wine often sets the mood for us. Those speaking from the Other Side have the uncanny knack of hitting you with the clear and undiluted truth right between the eyes! That kind of absolute honesty takes some getting used to. We are still working on that part.

Suddenly, after 10 years of extraordinary but primarily *voice* communications with the Other Side, *"Parting Notes"* started with a simple *written* instruction to me.

"There is someone here with a letter. Fetch me a paper."

And so the stream of parting notes began. Individuals and groups on the Other Side who wanted to tell us what it is like for them there each lined up to write one last letter. The full body deep trance voice mediumship continued but the letters took center stage.

All those who have written from the Other Side have their own reasons and their own message. Physical "death" it seems, like physical life, is quite an individual and rich experience. The descriptions of the dying process and of what it is like on the Other Side are not sugar coated. Not by a long shot. The truth never is. However, they all have something in common. There is something about the Other Side that you can count on, something that is comforting. It is uplifting just to know that indeed there is an "Other Side".

The story of Sarah was written by our friends on the Other Side after I had asked them for an introduction to the letters. I was thinking of a brief one or two paragraph introduction explaining who they were and a little something about the death and dying process from their points of view. What was given was more and completely different than what I expected (as usual). Within the story of Sarah finding the letters is as profound an introduction, not just to the letters, but also to the whole subject of death, dying and life-after-death as I could ever have hoped for. It is suitable for people of all ages. Also, who's to say that the Sarah story might not someday come true in our future? Time, as they say on the Other Side, "is a curious thing."

The story of Sarah finding the letters was written via the medium in handwritten form just like the forward to this book and the letters themselves. Every word (other than this introduction, and some clearly marked "notes" that I have added) is presented exactly as first written by those on the Other Side, word-for-word in the first, final, and only draft.

There is no editing whatsoever of the communications except for a very occasional spelling correction, primarily of the word "existence" that for some reason was almost always spelled "existance" in the letters. Even so, if the "writers" on the Other Side chose to write "my self" instead of "myself", as is often the case, or if we thought that their use of slang or a particular spelling of a word, or use of "who" instead of "whom" might have reflected a local time, place, level of education, or just their mood or personality, their usages were left unchanged by us.

Unlike the voice communications, when the letters are written it is not interactive. They just come and then they are gone. The medium has no memory of them other than a dream-like recollection that very quickly fades. April is often quite surprised afterwards when she reads what has been written by someone else using her hand while she was "out". For me it is simply riveting to watch each word appear on the page not knowing where the thread will lead or when it will be complete.

These communications were written from the Other Side of the veil with love via a very talented trance medium for an important purpose, of that I am sure. They have expanded my own understanding and awareness immensely and for that I am eternally honored and grateful to my wife April and to those on the Other Side who chose to write them. This is a true account, although only a partial one, of my life married to a trance medium. There's more. Much more.

Allen Crawford

Part I

An Introductory Story: From the Other Side

Sarah Crawford

The sun rose as usual on that September morning. Amid the rising neighborhood all of the same patterns were followed by the family of Sarah Crawford. An alarm clock summoned the awakening of the family. Sarah's mother stumbling sleepily to the kitchen to brew a pot of coffee. Sarah's dad pushing the snooze alarm then falling back to sleep. Jim + Derek the teens of the family and Sarah's older brothers ignoring their mother's pleas to rise and shine. Everything was as usual right down to Sparky the dog asking for a morning walk. That is everything except today was Grandma's funeral. Sarah lay wide-eyed in forbiddance in her frilly bedroom. Today she would say goodbye to the woman she loved most in the world. Grandma. Grandma who made the best sugar cookies on the planet. Grandma who read stories to you way past bedtime. Grandma with her sparkly blue eyes and beautiful fingernails of which she was most proud. Gone all of it. Gone with the mis-beat of a heart that allowed a blood clot to take Grandma away forever.

Sarah pulled the covers up to her chin. September had brought with it a slight chill. The extra blankets felt warm and comfortable to Sarah. She was eleven years old. Her hair a lovely shade of auburn. A slightly tipped nose with cute freckles. Sarah hated those freckles.

3

However, they did not seem to be fading anytime soon so she was learning to live with them.

Holding her breath under the blanket Sarah tried to imagine death. What had it been like for Grandma? Was she scared when it happened? She would really like to know and wished Grandma could tell her somehow. A small tear slid down her cheek as she recalled her last visit with Grandma.

The Visit

Grandma's kitchen was the best place for a little girl to be. The air rich with the scent of vanilla always beckoned Sarah. There were jars of freshly baked cookies and treats. A little pot of something brewing constantly on the stove. It seemed like a dollhouse to Sarah. Frilly curtains with antique table + chairs. Everything was embroidered with bright colored thread and love.

Grandma cherished the time she could spend with her beloved grandchild. In her older years she had learned an appreciation of family and was dedicated to those she loved.

Sarah spent many weekends with grandma puttering around the garden, baking cookies and learning about spiritual things.

The spiritual things were their little secret. Not many people know what Grandma was able to do. Sarah knew. And on that last visit a torch was passed to a new generation. The gift of psychic

4

channeling. Sarah had been guided for years at the art of spiritual communication. Of course she always thought of it as a fun game. Grandma talking with and for people who were not there. The rest of the family thought Grandma a little out there but Sarah loved her more than ever. She was proud to be included in anything Grandma was doing.

While in the garden they came across a dead squirrel. There were no apparent causes for death. Just a limp body stretched out reaching for some flowers.

"Why is the squirrel dead?" asked Sarah.

Grandma replied, "The squirrel has gone back to the source of all things. It passed while frolicking in the garden."

"Did it hurt?" asked Sarah.

"No, my dear, death comes in the blink of an eye. One barley notices until a guide points it out."

"Oh" replied Sarah, not quite convinced. Looking down at the poor creature Sarah could not help wondering if death really did hurt. Sure all of the spiritual guides she had spoken to through Grandma spoke of death as an easy natural thing but most of them had never been in a physical body. So what did *they* know?

They held a miniature funeral for the creature. A shoebox served as a coffin and it was buried among the flowers it loved. Hand in hand Grandma + Sarah walked back to the house that day. Many questions of death still ran through Sarah's mind. However, being a child she was able to put aside those kinds of thoughts while munching on some of Grandma's special cookies.

Looking back, the smell of cookies always brought times with Grandma back to Sarah. Now she was gone and nothing would ever be the same.

The Funeral

Everyone dressed in black, as a family in mourning should do. Looking uncomfortable in a seldom worn suit Sara's Dad herded everyone to the car. It too was black. A stark contrast to the beautiful sunlight of that September day. And a complete reverse of what Grandma was. She was anything but somber. This was to be a traditional burial. There were three days at the funeral home with Grandma lying in her coffin, then onto a church service and then to the cemetery. Sarah was horrified. Grandma would never have agreed to this. She must do something! As her mother stepped from the car Sarah stepped up beside her.

"Mom"? Sarah said.

"Shh...what is it Sarah"

"Grandma would not have liked this much. She always said she wanted to be cremated and spread to the wind. Why are you doing this?"

Sarah's mom took a deep breath and replied. "Because this is what your father wants and what he thinks is right. Now let's get into the church before the service begins."

Sarah obeyed her mother but was filled with sadness that Grandma might be watching and would be disappointed. No one ever understood Grandma like Sarah did. Even her own son had thought she was misled in her beliefs.

Throughout the service Sarah kept hoping for a sign. The afterlife was a magical place according to her Grandma. At least she would honor Grandma and would never forget what she had taught her.

The relief after the cemetery was immense. They had gotten through the worst of it. Now there was only having to leave without Grandma. That task would eventually be easier for the others but not for Sarah.

The lights of her home were warm + inviting that evening. Sarah went to her room and wondered about Grandma. Was she at peace? Did she feel weird without her body? She really wished she could talk to her. Alas she knew no one who could do what her Grandma did. Silently Sarah began to sob trying to release the pain she felt in her heart.

There was a light tap at the door. Her father entered the room + sat at the edge of her bed.

"Sarah"?

"Hi Daddy."

"Are you alright? You've been troubled all day."

"Daddy did it hurt for Grandma to die? I'm so worried about her. I wish I could talk to her."

"Look Sarah I know your Grandma had some pretty wild ideas. She used to tell me all those crazy stories too. I just never believed her like you do. Grandma is fine. She'll be waiting for you in heaven."

Sarah thought a moment then boldly replied. "Daddy you know there is no distinct heaven. It's where you create it."

Her Dad sighed and replied. "I guess she converted you huh? Well sweetie beliefs are your own personal thing. I did however want to give you something that Grandma left for you. She was going to give it to you when you were older but now seems like a good time. I'm not sure what it is but please take it!"

He handed her a cigar box. Tattered and worn the edges frayed with time. There was an aroma to it that smelled like Grandma's house. By closing her eyes Sarah was able to imagine herself with her again. She held the box close and breathed deeply.

Curiosity caused Sarah to turn the box over after her father left. It was taped shut with plain scotch tape. Using her fingernails Sarah was able to pick off the tape + open the box.

Inside there was nothing but paper. Sarah was surprised that Grandma would leave her something so odd. Upon closer inspection she saw that the paper was very old and that on each sheet was a letter.

Would these be love letters from an old beau? Sarah decided it would make her feel closer to Grandma to read them. So she curled up in her bed to do some reading. Love letters indeed!

The Box

The box was ordinary. A cigar box with stories to tell. The edges worn, while the top still fitting securely wiggled slightly when opened. Sarah lifted it to her nose and inhaled deeply. It smelled like Grandma. The aroma brought back memories that flooded her like a waterfall. Not knowing whether to laugh or cry Sarah opened the lid. There was a stack of papers neatly folded in different colors. Each one beckoned with promises of enlightenment. Perhaps they were not love letters sent to Grandma when she was a girl. There were more than a hundred in all. Folded thoughtfully by some ardent writer with a story to tell. Sarah held them close in hopes of catching a hug from her. They were probably pieces of information that Grandma wrote down over the years. She was great on thought and spiritual insights. As a channel there was a great amount of information that Grandma thought was important. Hopefully there would be a note of encouragement. Sarah could use that right now.

On the top of the stack was a note card. On the front an angel was pictured. A tear fell from Sarah's eyes as she gazed upon it. Now Grandma was an angel. Lingering over the picture it was a while before Sarah opened the note card. Printed neatly was a letter of sorts. When she first read it Sarah was unsure of its meaning. It took a few moments for the words to sink in.

MY DEAREST SARAH,

I HAVE LEFT YOU WITH THE ANSWERS TO THE QUESTIONS YOUR ARE NOW ASKING. YOU HAVE ENCOUNTERED THE SPIRIT WORLD WITH ME MANY TIMES. I AM AWARE OF YOUR MISGIVINGS AND THOUGHTS NOW. THE LAST PHYSICAL THING I CAN GIVE YOU IS PEACE. THESE LETTERS WILL GIVE YOU THAT. THEY WILL ALSO GIVE YOU PERSPECTIVE ABOUT LIFE AND DEATH. KEEP THEM AS A REFERENCE. YOUR CHILDREN WILL ALSO WANT TO KNOW. DEATH IS A UNIVERSAL QUESTION. ONE THAT ALL WILL DESIRE AN ANSWER TO. READ THESE AND KNOW I EXIST. IN THAT EXISTENCE WE WILL CONTINUE OUR CLOSENESS.

LOVE

GRANDMA

PS: READ THEM WITH AN OPEN HEART. THEY WERE WRITTEN WITH AN OPEN SPIRIT.

The First Letter

The sun had dipped under the horizon when Sarah finished her letter from Grandma. She felt frozen in time as she held the sheet in her hand. All the memories came back of the funeral and Sarah realized the finality of it all. Tears splashed upon the ink causing some of the letters to blend together. It didn't matter the words were forever seared into her heart. It was amazing how intuitive her grandmother had been. No one else would be able to foresee the questions that would need to be answered after her death. And Grandma had seen that Sarah would not be left alone and full of questions. How like her!

Sarah took a tissue, blew her nose and wiped her eyes. She would need to have her full wits about her when she read the letters. Her nose red, her eyes puffy but eager she picked up the first letter. Where did Grandma get these letters and what did they reveal? There had been some very strange sessions where Grandma had claimed to be in touch with the recently deceased. Being a channel was considered a trendy thing at the end of the 20th century. There were a lot of charlatans + wannabe's.

It never seemed to Sarah that Grandma had participated in a fad. She was far too reverent for that. Sarah had talked to entities while Grandma was in trance. She never found it unusual. Then again, she never found Grandma unusual. Now she wondered who she had actually spoken to on those occasions. It didn't matter now. All she had left was this box of letters and a void that needed to be filled.

Sarah opened the letter. Expecting something yet nothing, she began to read.

Dear Sarah,

You do not know us by name. We exist in the peripheral of physical life. The opportunity afforded to us by your grandmother was indeed a precious gift. There are many levels of living. Each important in its own right. All the levels are accessible but communication between them not always available. Souls traveling together sometimes get separated. Without your grandmother's assistance messages of encouragement solace and love cannot jump the barrier. Look not at her with suspicion or amusement. All that she is about to reveal to you is true. You knew of some of the communication but not of its depth. You are about to be enlightened. All of us anticipated your arrival. Read these gifts your grandmother allowed us to give. We are all alive and well. We only wish to share the marvel of all existence. Each of these letters will alter one person's life, or perhaps many in unison. After you have read them, share them. That was the intent in which they were written. All exist because of your grandmother.

Read with love.
All of us.

Sarah looked into the box. It was filled with notes and letters. All of them were dated and obviously were written over a period of time. She did not bother to count them. She could feel a warmth caressing her as she undid the first bundle. These letters were from dead people. Grandma sure could get ya even in death. Sarah laughed and opened the first sheet. This was going to be something.

Part II

"There is someone here with a letter.

Fetch the paper..."

Thomas Johnson

Dear friend,

Aside from the usual trappings of death, I have made a startling discovery. The "I" still survives. I am aware of a blend of others but my thoughts remain distinct. A ripple of laughter escapes and I feel jolly. Not exactly what one would expect when finding the definition of self at risk. In the last moments of my "life" I was so fearful of annihilation. So fearful that my thoughts not recorded would be forever lost in oblivion. I raced to leave a legacy. Now I see the absurdity of it all. Everything comes with you. Everything. Even the little irritants of one's personality that most likely would have been better off in oblivion. My, My, My. I can see all the experiences and the several strings of continuity connecting them all. That life to which I obsessively clung to was a fraction of the whole picture. To hold on to it would have robbed me of the universal plan. The plan I designed so long ago.

The opportunity to write some thoughts after "death" was sweet. I wish for many things but the one true thing that sets my soul afire is talking to you. I could be anyone that you know. The act of spiritual communication is a real thing. Something like this needs to be taken from the side show forum to mainstream.

I feel determination to see this occur. My growth would have been altered by such a thing. My soul feels expansion by knowing a physical person reads my thoughts. The thoughts of a dead man are valuable. The creation of a map to the hereafter is now available. I will continue my communications because it is the next step in my evolution. I feel honor at the opportunity to be a part of yours. You too shall prevail in the hereafter. The body will turn to dust but it is only a costume for the real you. That which you perceive as you inside your head will remain. It is true. I am proof.

Thomas Johnson

Dear friend,

Aside from the usual trappings of death, I have made a startling discovery. The "I" still survives.

...

to be a part of yours. You too once will be in the here after. Your The body will turn to dust but it is only a costume for the real you. That which you perceive as you inside your head will remain. It is true.—I am proof.

Thomas Johnson

I Was Dead, Yet I Still Was

Dear friend

I write with awe and genuine surprise. Spending this last existence totally convinced there was not a divine afterlife. I now rescind those thoughts.

I was an average guy going about my daily life in the usual manner. I lived on 33'rd street in NYC. I was a fashion assistant and led a pretty avant-garde lifestyle. There was a mix of friends from various backgrounds. We all lived life in the moment. I do not know why they did. I do know why I did. I believed that this was all we had, this life. There was not any of the propaganda that so many religious groups preach of. I believed that once you died it was over. Completely over. So in my average way I lived as avant-garde as I could. Always I reached for that little bit more. I learned of my illness in my thirty seventh year. It had a very long name but it zeroed in on one thing. Death. My death. Of course I scurried from one doctor to another searching for a reprieve to my death sentence.

I didn't get one. Angry at my fate I lived as furiously as I could. Denial was my best friend. Well meaning associates asked if I needed guidance. For what!? I was going to die. It would be over. Kaput! As the disease took over my body every day became a precious gift. I realized that I was saddened by the finality of it. Never did I expect what I encountered at the end.

The last day was filled with pain. The pain killers were wearing thin. Not wanting to be delirious I refused more medication. I wanted to be coherent in those last moments. My best friend Chad sat with me. He spoke of God, heaven and eternal life. I wanted to tell him what bullshit that all was but it seemed to comfort him so I left it alone. He started to pray and begged me to join him. I refused. There was nothing to pray for, the show was over. I closed my eyes becoming lulled by the tone of his voice. I don't remember when it changed but suddenly it wasn't Chad anymore. There was someone new beside me. Perhaps I had dozed off and a new vigilant had come to sit with me.

I opened my eyes. There was a moment of blurriness then I focused on the most beautiful blue eyes I had ever seen. They seemed to dance in waves like the ocean. The ocean sparked a memory of a time long past in my childhood when I felt safe and full of life. I did not recognize the person but the eyes filled me with a sense of home. I should have felt weak but I wanted to throw back the covers and run to the beach. And I did. This person followed me at a distance ever watchful. I felt that he was protecting me. The waterfront was far away but I arrived in seconds. The water lapping up against my calves felt great. I stood there for a long time just looking at the horizon reveling in all its beauty & possibilities.

My vigilant friend came to my side and stood with me. It dawned on me who it was. My shock made me unable to speak for many moments. This person was angelic. I was dead, yet I still was. My eyes filled with tears at my lack of belief. I had been so mistaken. Now I was to be forgiven for my lack. The ocean enveloped me like the arms of my friend. The circle of love I had fought so desperately was now complete. No matter what you think there is more. The only one fooled is yourself if you believe there is nothing more. It is the one belief that will not come true.

Me.

Theodore

Dear friend,

I miss the common pattern of living. The usual quirks and rhythms one creates while moving through development and finally into adulthood. I always carried a love for Grape soda from the time I could hold the bottle on my own. The images conjured through the frosty bottle down to the last flavorful sip always relaxed me right down to my core essence. In retrospect for me to categorize life patterns through Grape soda seems rather ridiculous. However even now the thought is a comfort. I know I have lived many times, evolution's the main thread throughout. Each time however in the last phases I found myself forgetful and fearful of what is about to happen. Again + again I shake my head at the absurdity of the fear. I know the not remembering a life is critical to the process but it seems somehow a bit unfair. Why not know?

There are of course many arguments on the subject + those more evolved than I debate them eternally. However this is my note to you. I choose to tell you that it is nothing. A stroke of midnight, a whisper of

27

wind through the trees. No matter what pain the physical present presents the end result is serene and beautiful. It has never been otherwise for me.

As I page through the epitaph of my lives I find that my taste for Grape soda evolved from gaul an early Altaic drink. I much prefer the grape soda.

I will soon begin again. The pattern of living beacons me and I've more exploring to do. My main concern is to find an ample supply of grape soda for my journey. Sounds ridiculous? Only to those who do not know how to create what they want.

Perchance we will meet. Buy me a soda + we will toast to the process now that you have had a first hand account.

Theodore

Darryl

July 5, 1917

Dear Friend

It is my greatest hope that this note finds its way to you. I have traveled far since our last communication. The desire fills my soul so that it overflows onto this parchment with vivid expression of my devotion. Therefore it was with great concern that I embarked on this final journey without so much as a farewell. Perhaps the heavens will be merciful and allow this note to ease the burden of what I am about to tell you.

A few weeks hence I found myself on a train to Brussels. The unit I was assigned to was to report there for instructions. However the journey was cut short by an explosion, which impeded the train's arrival to the station. The precise moment still rings in my ears and the quick lurch of the car shall forever be engrained in my memory. Bodies and suitcases mingled together in a giant toss of energy. I cannot recall if the pain rendered me unconscious or the sheer surprise of being airborne stopped my heart cold in my chest. The final impact against the steel wall was not felt I assure you.

For a brief moment I looked around at the display of human carnage. Under regular circumstances I would have been sickened. On the contrary I found myself examining the scene with out a quiver. My poor body was a shambles. Amazing how frail it was. The design so delicate. I stepped through the door of the car and found that I was most likely the only one alive. There was not a single whisper of life, only the remaining fumes of gas and the remnants of twisted metal. Looking up I could see the sun shining as it reflected off the mangled sides of the train. It was truly beautiful. An artful masterpiece. There seemed to be a spectacular show of lights as some of the train began to implode upon itself. That's when I decided to write to you so you would not worry. I am quite fine. Different but fine.

As the train caught fire it disturbed me that my letter would be destroyed if I left it with the body. Therefore, I walked all day to the next village so that it would post to you straight away. As you can see, desire can create miracles.

The sun is setting and I must continue my journey. I'm not sure of the final destination but I am going any ways. Know that I am thinking of you. Thought continues though the body may not. Keep this letter with you as a reminder of the wonder of desire.

     All my Love
        Darryl.

Darryl died July 5, 1917 - his friend received this letter July 11th, through the post, 10 miles from the train wreck

T

Dear friend

The sky opens to meet me. Odd how that occurs when one truly looks. I spent many years gazing at the sky. Never did I realize the expansiveness of its existence. My error occurred when I tried to see with my eyes instead of my soul. Upon my death those spiritual eyes suddenly grasped the enormity of the universe. Each breath taken after death placed me in a vortex of energy that far surpassed anything I knew. The vastness of what we call the cosmos out runs my pretext of words. I truly do not think there is adequate vocabulary to describe it. There was a moment where I thought of declining this communication, as the language is inadequate. However the need for any communication supercedes the quality. Thus I write in this primitive tongue to you dear friend.

I realize how the arrogance creeps in but alas it is time. My mind now filled with many languages all of which I spoke at one time or another.

If possible move past that moment to the truths that I bring you. There is a level of existence that encompasses more than you can comprehend. Now that I have left my physical form I can embrace that existence and become one with it. In the physical we are preoccupied with physical needs. Sometimes those needs help us evolve other times they serve as a distraction. I now see the whole picture. We communicate to open your eyes. Spiritually or physically to another way of living. And we desire to comfort any fears that you associate with the end of physical existence. It simply does not apply to the vastness of your soul. Our goal is to communicate this. There is no other purpose.

We give you our word as spiritual beings that we speak the truth. For as spiritual beings the truth is all there is. No drama exists here. It is petty and unworthy of the richness of this plane. Close your eyes and visualize if you desire a place beyond any expectation. If you can create it in your mind multiply it by a thousand fold. That is where you will be when the physical is shed and you become your true self.

T

What It's Like To Die

Dear friend

In our lifetime we often dwell upon what it would be like to die. Is it scary? Does it hurt? Will I realize what is happening to me? All these are legitimate questions that in life we feel are left unanswered or to chance. It is definitely in your realm of control. At least most of the time. How you experience death is linked mostly with your emotional & Spiritual state at the time of death. In my case this time I was surrounded by loved ones and was at peace with the way my life had progressed. I was accepting and ready to go home so to speak. I had cancer, which caused considerable pain and a multitude of drugs for relief. The cancer was a manifestation of issues unresolved. I won't go into details about the cancer though. It is personal in nature and does not have anything to do with the act of transition through death.

This recitation is merely a look at or experience of the transition. I knew my physical body was failing miserably. I can still hear my heart pounding in my chest as the last moments came. The anticipation was so much worse. I calmed myself with the love I felt from my friends & family who came to see me off. I concentrated on my breath. In. Out. In. Out. As I began to shut down I stiffened in fear but forced my self to relax. Having read all the books about the light and the tunnel I kept my eyes open awaiting a vision.

However it was much different than what I thought. Perhaps the drugs they were giving me for pain enhanced the moments. I am not sure. Nonetheless I remember inhaling, looking into the eyes of all those I loved. Upon exhaling all of the faces blended into ones that I still knew but were different. I realized that these "new" faces were those of ones I had known before. There was not a blinding light nor a tunnel merely a change of scenery. I can remember wondering when I would finally be dead. I looked around at the faces before me and asked. I was told that the transition had occurred and I was now "alive" not dead. They likened it to a snake shedding its skin, merely a "wrap" that no longer was of use. I turned around hoping for a glimpse of my former self but it was gone. Only existing now in my memory.

Expecting to feel remorse I was surprised when the only feeling I had was joy. There was no pain and all my parts seemed to be in working order. My friends greeted me with a warmth forgotten in the bonds of physical. I was home.

There is so much to do and ponder. If I said that every moment was filled I would be a liar. Moments no longer have measurement. Each one lingers and becomes part of me expanding my perception beyond anything in the physical. So you see my friend there is adventure awaiting you. Fear not. Accept and surrender to something that has served all of us forever.

My experience is unique as yours will be. There are many more of us willing to share our experience in hopes it will give you courage in yours.

Me

Amelia

Dear friend

The sensations of death still ripple through that which I still consider me. In life the essence of death was an enigma to me. Not having very much experience on the subject I would have appreciated some insight.

The idea of death is shrouded in black and foreboding. How unfortunate. I found it to be one of the most physically bright events I ever experienced.

My step into the void was abrupt, the full thought of it escapes me as the initial moments of eternity engulfed me. Everything resounded with joy and lightness. I had hoped for a reunion, and was not disappointed.

It was not painful. Propaganda to the contrary was always a fear of mine. In fact once the last breath escaped my lips there was a definite uplifting feeling. I suppose the best way to describe it would be to compare it to this. Imagine yourself in the deep end of a pool of water. You are at the deepest point. You are about to run out of air. You push off the bottom and feel the surge of energy as you rise to the top. You are

37

about to run out of air as you break through into the air. The blue sky awaits you. Air sucked deeply into your lungs feels like nectar. As you exhale the exuberance of life envelops you. It is the same in death, only this time the exhilaration is not fleeting. It builds.

We speak so that you can remove the shadow of fear. We speak to lead you to forever. We also speak for those who cannot or will not. We appreciate the opportunity. That being a gift itself.

Your experience will be enhanced without the fear. There are others with different stories. We hope you resonate with one.

Peace + Love

Amelia

Hector

Dear friend

I remember the barrel of the gun feeling like a cold penny against my forehead. The rough grip of calloused hands as they forced me to the floor. The dust of the wooden floor went up my nose and for a brief second I thought I would sneeze. One never knows when one will look death in the eye. It creeps up slowly and jumps out in front of you in between breaths. I never expected that October morning that it would be my last. The sun came up just like any other day. The rooster crowing kicking me out of bed at first light. The house was always very cold til someone stoked the fire. Since I was the daddy that would be my job. Everyday pretty much the same. Sharecropping land my daddy was enslaved to. There wasn't much money but it was a freeman's living. To us it was the most important. We dreamed of better for our children. In the meantime we did what we had to do.

That particular morning I was going to town. I had some eggs to sell and I was gonna surprise Ester my wife with a little sugar to bake with. She did so love to bake, especially sweet things.

39

I hooked up the wagon and headed on out. This morning especially extra special. The air was crisp and the leaf color was at its peak. I took my time. It was rare I got the chance to ponder a little. The ride to town was quicker than what I would have liked.

I stopped first at the market to sell the eggs. There were 13 of them. Just enough for 2 penny worth. I had dealt with Ezra the shop keeper before and he was usually fair. I set the basket of eggs on the counter. There was a white man in front of me. It wouldn't have mattered if he was behind me. I would have to wait till all the white folk had their turn. That was allright. I was a patient man.

This time however the white man took offense at my setting the basket by him. He began to drop the eggs on the floor one at a time. Watching my 2 cents turn to mush on the floor extracted a sigh from my throat. Big mistake. I never had time to exhale before the floor came up to greet me. The muzzle of the gun at my head. I closed my eyes in hope that if I thought + prayed hard enough time would stop and everything would be allright.

The taunting voice ringing in my ears, telling me that I didn't seem to know my place. Oh god I did. I did know my place. The hammer of the trigger echoing in my ears. My eyes squeezed shut trying to pray, trying to beg my way back to life. I didn't hear the sound nor did I feel the bullet. I tried to open my eyes but they were filled with Ester making pie on Sunday. The leaves were orange and red and the first snow was building in the sky. It would be Christmas soon. I would have to kill the old hen for dinner. Ester sure made a fine holiday dinner.

I could hear shouts above me. The dust from the floor got stuck in the corners of my mouth. My throat parched from extra air. I would have to get a drink as soon as I got my 2 cents. There was a trough outside. Wasn't there? I forgot. Drums pounded in different levels. I never realized the beat & rhythm of shoes as they hit the floor. It was melodic and reminded me of stories I had heard about Africa.

I felt a kick in my back which reminded me of how my pa whooped me when I was twelve for lying. Vaguely I heard the word "dead" from somewhere. It just didn't seem important. I looked over my shoulder and there was my daddy. He looked just like he did when I was a boy. His hand on my shoulder brought tears to my eyes. It was good to feel his warmth again. I didn't realize how much I missed it. He asked me if I was thirsty. When I replied "Yes Sir" he clapped me on the back and said "I know a right fine watering hole let's you and me go get us a brew".

It never occurred to me that I had never been old enough when he was alive to have "a brew" with him. I accepted his hand and off we went.

I looked back at my eggs all smashed on the floor. Part of me was still there too. On my father's arm it just didn't seem all that important. My only concern was Ester. What about her? "She'll be along," replied my father.

So off we went making plans to live on. Ester joined us a while later and I gave her the sugar I had always wanted to give her. There was no pain, no sorrow, only joy. We write to let someone know. We live on and we are happy.

HECTOR

Dear friend

I remember the barrel of the gun feeling like a cold penny against my forehead. The rough grip of calloused hands as they forced me to the .. the dust on the wooden floor went up my .. .. I would

...

There was no pain, no sorrow. We write to let someone know. We live on and we are happy.

HECTOR

Rachel

Dear friend,

It is said that the last moments of life are the most dear. It is then that the soul savors the last bit of physicality. Your life runs before your eyes like a silent film. Events rise & fall in a crescendo of emotion.

I can tell you that most of it is true. You see I am what you would term as dead. I can still communicate however, certainly a surprise for me.

I always believed that once you died it was over. Now I know different.

The last glimmer of life left my body in the evening. I was disappointed because I wanted to see the morning sun one more time. There were many things I regretted leaving behind. My last intake of breath was painful, the exhale oddly soothing. I expected panic but remained calm. My body stopped functioning but my spirit became more acute. It was odd.

Images passed before me. My eyes no longer available I began to use thought as an indicator to what I perceived. I found the images to be sharper. Very odd. Of course there was a ripple of chaos when everyone realized I was dead.

Their tears such a waste for I was more alive than before. I hoped for language skills of any sort so that I could convey I was OK. I soon learned that a spiritual connector was needed for such things. Now at last it has revealed itself to me. And now I speak. No easy task without a body of your own.

My message is simple. "You live on." In an altered state but alive. I know that it would have been important for me to know that when I was alive in the physical. I hope it gives you comfort. Without a physical body it is different. One learns to create what one needs. Perhaps creation is a process to be practiced. Just know that all is well. Go in peace and love.

Rachel

Dear friend,

It is said that the last moments of life are the most dear. It is then that the Soul savors the last bit of physicality. Your life runs before your eyes like a silent film. Events rise & fall in a crescendo of emotion.

I can tell you that most of it is true. You see I am what you would term as dead. I can still communicate however. Certainly a surprise for me.

...

it would have been important for me to know that when I was alive in the physical. I hope it gives you comfort. Without a physical body it is different. One learns to create what one needs. Perhaps creation is a process to be practiced. Just know that all is well. Go in peace and love

Rachel

I Write This Letter From Another Place

Dear friend

I always had a fear of death. From the time I could walk the idea piqued my interest. What would it feel like when I actually took the last breath? Not really a subject a child should be pondering. I was told repeatedly by my parents to stop putting those thoughts in front of me. They endeavored to distract me by filling my life with learning, sports and activities. Luckily it worked because every small child appreciates distraction especially when it revolves around them. Ultimately I put my thoughts to other things, at least until I was a teenager.

Puberty hit me like a diesel engine. Suddenly hormones drove my every movement. A passing member of the opposite sex served as a potentially major distraction for everything I was supposed to be doing. I obviously fell in love with the first girl who paid me any attention and proceeded to explore my sexuality. At that time that was all there was in my existence. It seemed it would endure forever.

Everything came to a crashing halt when my true love was killed in an automobile accident. The finality of it caused my belief in my own immortality to falter. Now there was a reason to wonder again what happened. The drama catapulted me right back to the question of what it felt like. Did she suffer? Was she scared? Did she know? All of these questions left without answers plagued me my whole remaining life.

I awaited my own death with a perverse anticipation. My parents would have been appalled at my fascination. Both of them died without me at their side. I wish I had been there the precise moment so that I could have asked them what they were experiencing. I became obsessed with death thereafter.

I write this letter from another place in hopes that there may be another with the same questions as I. Perhaps this letter will answer some long awaited question by someone who needs to know what does it feel like to die?

Since I have already answered that question for my self I am eager to share my experience.

There is no need to fear. I was "killed in an accident caused by a diesel truck. The car I was driving was hit almost head on when it jumped a center meridian on the freeway. The initial knowledge that it was going to hit me did cause the adrenaline to pass through my heart. It was so quick that I barely had time to panic. I was frozen behind the wheel of my car. I closed my eyes just in time. I remember a very loud bang then a hissing sound like all of the air in front of me was being sucked away. I felt my body stop against a hard surface. I waited for the truck to hit knowing it was going to hurt like hell. Death did not occur to me! After a few moments I opened my eyes. Everything around me was in chaos but I felt strangely calm. There were people running everywhere in panic. There was fear that the truck would explode and there were 2 guys trying to pull a man from a smoldering piece of metal. Upon closer inspection I realized it was a car. There wasn't much left of it and the poor guy inside must have been dead. Nonetheless I ran to them to help.

There was a lot of screaming as the two guys tried to pry open the door. Unfortunately it was seared shut. Pounding on the window it was determined that the guy inside was most likely dead. The fire department arrived and everyone was trying to get this poor guy out. Puzzled I moved forward and easily slipped inside the wreckage. It made me wonder what the problem was. It seemed odd that getting inside was so easy for me. Those other guys must be idiots. I touched the shoulder of the man. His body was still warm. Maybe he was still alive after all. The adrenaline feeling came again when I pulled him back to reveal his face. It was me. Or at least my identical twin.

I started to laugh. It was a deep belly laugh that I had not experienced for many years. I was dead! I had died in a horrible accident and it was over. There was nothing to fear. Only my own self imposed thoughts.

So you see, death will come but not annihilation. What ever the experience is there will be a moment for you to look back on it like any other experience you've had. If I had known this it would have impacted my life. Thus the reason for this letter. Hopefully it will impact you in some positive way.

Go in peace

Me

Death Is Not What You Would Think

Dear friend

I have attempted to communicate my thoughts on so many occasions. The frustration of not getting through has dampened my spirits. Imagine the appreciation I feel at this opportunity. We were taught as children that death is an ascension to God. Indeed it is. However the ascension is vibratory in nature. Hence the inability to speak to you as I would wish. Knowing the contact must come from myself, I have relentlessly pursued one who could adjust vibrations so that they could be understood. Here we are blended as one so that I may speak.

There were many so called adventures attached to this letter. It began with my end so to speak. Death is not what you would think. It is nothing like anything we were taught. All the stories were designed to give a unified appearance so that we would not be fearful. The gates of heaven with St. Peter residing and a host of other myths propagated by the various religions of our species. All of them too broad, too generalized, too easy. Death is a beginning and that beginning is very individualized. Again we are the masters of death as

53

we are the masters of our lives. Nothing changes. I could detail my experiences but they would not be truth for you. For you are the only one who holds the ability to create your transition. It is your adventure. In this knowledge it would be prudent to ponder your perception of death and ascension to a new vibratory status. One thing for certain is that death is personal and is what you make of it just as in physical life.

Think on that a while.

Me

We must retain our vibration level so a measure of time is limited so that we may speak. Now that we have found a keyhole we the key shall return for more interaction.

Appolonius	Sri Kante
Bintu	Verislaus
phillippe	Calrin

We must retain our vibration level so
a measure of time is limited So that we
my speak. Now that we have found a keyhole
we the key shall return for more interaction

Appolonius   Sir Kente
Bintu   Verislaus
phillippe   Calvin

Sarah Bradley 1867

How long I have waited for a moment such as this. I am Sarah. I am American. Please listen. The day of my death seems a breath away tho I know time is longer. I fell off a wagon during a land run. Oklahoma territtory the year of our Lord 1867 Please tell those left behind I miss them. They would be Bradleys. My father was a blacksmith, I know he no longer lives but I have not mingled with him. He has issues to work with. The bible of my momma is buried in the grave. The stories are a comfort but not within any meaning of the heaven after life.

I could go on to another place tho I do not wish to. So I wait. The letter to you is more important. You should know there is no hell. No devil. No fire. No brimstone. My parents were mistaken. A clean soul is an informed one, which is my purpose.

I fell from the wagon a baptised child of God I am here as a grown up child of the heavens. God is in my very touch. God has always been with me. Not in a church or history book. Tell others I am happy. Tell the others to live according to the whispers they hear on silent nights. Tell others that a fall from a wagon is a painless one diredtly to the arms of themselves, God.

Sarah Bradley 127

Take A Moment To Believe In Something Fantastic

Dear friend

I am close enough to smell a faint trace of lilac upon the skin of the one who allows me to speak. This integration has been very interesting. My first thoughts were that of a suit of clothing just a bit too tight at the seams. My energy is crowded by hers but a cooperation has been formed. The thought of experience such as this would never have occurred to me when I was physical. This opportunity was nearly missed due to my lack of urgency. What would I have to say that would enlighten those who have not transitioned yet? It was only the match of energies that propelled me rather unwillingly to this spot.

Now that the moment is mine I feel a falter in my new found ability. I was told to tell my story if I wished or merely to garner experience so that I would grow. It was my choice. You see I lived a rather ordinary life. Nothing profound occurred that would give the appearance of anything important. I was born. I lived. I survived. I raised a family. What could I tell you of my death? Nothing spectacular. A cancer began to deteriorate my colon and that was it. I can remember turning my head to speak to my wife Sylvia but I simply could not move my lips any longer. I would have liked to tell her not to cry but I couldn't. It surprised me to be so lucid but not to be able to let anyone know I was allright.

I watched with fascination my funeral and ceremony. My body now was detached from what was really me. Not important, although I really thought my blue eyes were great. Silly thoughts but you do think of those things. I was greeted by an entourage of beings none of whom I recognized. My form or what I presumed to be me was changing rapidly. Oh not deterioration by any means. It was changing from identity to identity. I was told we all keep the experiences from all of our lives tucked away in our essence. Now that that essence was free of physical bonds those lives came to the forefront. It was unbelievable. I was asked what I had learned and what did I teach while physical. There was also interest in hearing of what fantastic that my life gave to the world. Overwhelmed I panicked by not knowing one thing that was extraordinary about my life. I guess that's how I ended up here in a too tight physical form writing this letter.

Not a punishment I assure you. Actually I chose to be here albeit unwillingly at first and am honored to be speaking with you. The fact that this has occurred is extraordinary. I never would have believed this while physical in this most recent life. I guess I was just too caught up in the routine to allow myself to believe that extraordinary things do exist.

While racking my brain, (well I guess that has no meaning now) but while attempting to discover what I had taught while living comes down to this. Always take a moment to believe in something fantastic. The barriers of routine and familiar are constricting to the soul. Remember the soul has always taken flight. It is what it knows, and will return to after each physical life. I know that now. This experience has taught me that I am extraordinary by mere virtue of blending for this letter. And so are you.

Me.

Hector: "Death Is Much Easier Than Birth"

Dear friend

It requires so much more energy to begin than it does to die. We forget the effort in the measured dramas we live. It is a truly more rigorous project. In conception there is the ambiguous future so wrought with desire and misfortune. All the choices yet to be made and each on a strenuous question. In death all the mistakes have been made. The final conquest is review. The review however painful has no hope of reprisal other than the lesson to do better the next time. Yes death is much easier than birth. We know for we have done it many times. For those of you blinded by the physical we offer this observation in hopes that it will spare you the fear of death.

We realize that our pitiful review may be biased but it is truthful nonetheless. Death is merely an ending to a drama played out in the hopes of development. It is a repeated process so do not despair.

Hector.

"Anytime there is growth in the spirit, there is joy throughout the cosmos. . ."

I Am Writing To You As A Gift

Dear friend

I am writing to you as a gift. A gift given in hopes that what I have to tell you will encourage you to continue on your path. In the twists and turns of life we often find ourselves far from the place we thought we would be.

Certainly in this past life there were many surprises that made my life full. One of those was you. Never did I plan on reproducing, let alone an exquisite person like yourself. You are the product of my life a conglomeration of all the energy I am. You are a form of reincarnation for me. I see myself in your eyes. My hope is that you will listen to what I tell you. Knowing you as I do I realize there is a chance you will dismiss this note as a gimmick or farce. We sincerely hope that will be untrue. We left abruptly we know. The accident or should I say my predetermined physical end did not allow me to be able to render a few last pieces of advice. I also know how much this disturbed you. So with that let me continue.

Always keep tucked in your heart my amazement of your talent. Being your biggest fan was a pleasure I will take with me throughout eternity. Let that amazement permeate your essence and allow it to grow. Do not let my death stifle your joy. Know that I have not ended merely evolved. I did not suffer physically and now that I have been able to communicate with you my heart suffers no longer. Keep the words of this note next to your heart. Whether you believe they are from me or not does not matter. The essence of my connection with you will become enhanced by reading this. Be joyful. We will meet again although perhaps in different circumstances. Go now and be wonderful. I am content. So should you be.

I love you.

Me

Physical Death Is The Beginning

Dear friend

I write to you from the beginning. I realize that to you death or the life force transition signifies the end. Your cultures as humans speak of life everlasting but you continue to mourn physical death. So I write to you to give you a visual of what is the truth of the matter. Physical death is the beginning. The beginning of the cycle created to allow one to evolve and grow in the chain of evolution. This process brings us closer to the source of all life. The source is the energy pattern you call God.

I have traveled the process many times. There are many lessons to learn and evolution does not come quickly or cheaply. We all have distinct issues and therefore create dramas so that we may understand them better. Through this understanding we change to become closer to energetic perfection. You assume that the physical birth is the beginning. It is not. By reincarnating you are actually at the end of a very lengthy process by which you are embarking on fulfillment of all the lessons learned through the physical. Because of the fact that in the physical one

65

becomes so enslaved to 3 dimensions death becomes an ominous foe.

I realize that this may appear as gibberish to your eyes, or that the subject matter may seem misconstrued. I implore you to consider the possibility that I am correct. Try for a moment to accept death as the beginning. Fear it not. I linger in this body only to ensure that the message is delivered. Your acceptance is not obligatory. My wish for communication is fulfilled. We salute your progress for reading this letter.

Me.

Issac: "It Was Christmas"

Dear friend,

It was Christmas. A time of family. A time of giving. A time for endings & beginnings. For me it was both of those. At the time though the end seemed to be all that I had. Desperately I clung to the end. There was a glimmer of hope inside me that thought if I didn't let go the end would dissolve.

I never spent much time thinking about the end. It was always off in the distance. Something that came upon others but never approached me. I would send condolences to those that were left behind. The appropriate gesture, the appropriate customs followed. The end came only to those others, not me.

Imagine my surprise when the end came. I could not comprehend what was happening to me. It was an accident that occurred while driving to do some Holiday shopping. I had finished everything but the greeting cards. They were at home waiting to be written. Just a few more items and I was finished. The roaring sound that preceded the blow was deafening. My hearing was my only sense that did not fail me. The shattering glass, the screeching of rubber, my own intake of breath. I heard them all. I saw, nothing, felt nothing. Nothing. I heard it all. Then there was silence, a very pure one.

It occurred to me that I might have fainted. I had never done so in the past but you never know. I tried to open my eyes but couldn't. They just didn't work anymore. This was the end. I wasn't ready. I refused to go. There seemed to be a tussle with end as it tried to overcome me. I refused. I tried to think my way out of it but kept slipping to the end. I wasn't really afraid, just mad. Mad that the end came so soon. Mad that I would miss Christmas and really mad that I would not be sending my greeting cards this year.

The end was about to descend upon me when I found myself suddenly in a room. No explanation for this occurrence it just was. In the room I found my greeting cards set neatly upon a plain table. The end would not win until I wrote out my greeting cards. A feeble victory but I wallowed in the power of it & began to write. The end waited patiently and I took my time. I wrote all the things I ever wanted to tell everyone. I printed each on out with a delicate hand. If I couldn't defeat the end at least it would come on my terms.

When the last envelope was sealed I turned to the end and stepped towards it. I guess it was time to be brave and accept the end. My only regret was that no one would read my cards. It would give me great comfort to know that all of my friends & family would have a final word from me.

Closing my eyes I accepted my fate. Nothing happened. There was not a terrible demise. No suffering & gnashing of teeth. I suddenly felt my body. A bit different but I felt it just the same. There was a speck in the distance that was turning into a new horizon. A beginning. An inner voice revealed that this was my new beginning.

Every beginning is preceded by an end. This was just one in a long chain of evolution. Moving now with a new ease and abandon I was proud of myself. I turned to look back at the end and saw something really remarkable. All of my cards had been delivered. And in that delivery each of the recipients also had a new beginning. Pretty cool.

Issac

Footnote

Issac was in a coma for several months after a fatal accident that occurred before Christmas. He died on April 5, 1996. When they went to clean out his apartment no Christmas cards were found. However in June of that year 25 of his friends & family received Christmas cards from him. All of them found it odd that it took so long to get them. Each of them found comfort in his notes and did not find it odd that they got the cards. They simply assumed that the US postal system was faulty. None of them noticed that there was no postage on the envelopes.

[Note that the "footnote" was received as part of the letter.]

Theresa

Dear friend,

I always said my heart would stop if anything happened to my children. These things and events of recent moments have changed my perception. Before I babble on let me tell you my name. I am Theresa. I have also been a Ben, Joe, Cerphan and Rebecca. These things I know separate the confusion for me that you are most likely feeling in this moment.

Let us begin at my moment of death. My wish is to give you a clear picture of these things I know. I was Teresa. I was a wife, mother and friend of many. I lived in Fuigi outside of Rome. The exact time is not so important. The essence of my story is more than important.

In my culture the woman was the central figure of the family. My purpose was to serve my husband, bear him children (preferably a son, many sons) and nurture those children to adulthood. This was to propagate our bloodline so that our family would live forever. I bore my husband seventeen children. It was what I was. Most women like myself wore out doing this, however being of strong stock I survived.

It was in the year 1917. My children ranged in age from 9 months to 23 years of age. The land was good, our harvest the best. My husband Roberto and I rejoiced in our prosperity. Our children were healthy. So many in our village had died of this sickness of the lung called tuberculosis. I was smiled upon by God for my children lived well.

The sun always poured itself though the window of my kitchen. I loved watching the sky come into light at the break of day. Amid the voices of the young ones I embraced each day with joy. That is until the morning the soldiers came. They appeared as ants crawling in unison out of an ant hill. All the same linked as though to one brain. I first saw them while getting water from the well. My heart stopped cold as my mind took inventory of my children.

Racing back to the house I gathered them inside. My ability to count escaped my panicked soul. I counted sixteen while searching for the last one. He was my oldest son Edwardo the apple of my eye. He was coming up the path in front of the house oblivious to the unfolding drama. My husband was at the north end of our farm. The soldiers approached from the south. I was alone in my stand. No one would touch my children.

I can still see the bloodshot eyes of the commander as he sarcastically called to the house. He had intercepted my son along with his men. They held Edwardo tightly amused at his attempts to free himself. The snake beckoned the head of the household to come forth. They began to hit my son. Since my husband was not there I stepped boldly into the door frame. Edwardo's bloody face empowered me. I ran blindly toward the commander striking him in the process. He laughed at my foolishness. Imagine my pleasure when his eyes widened in disbelief when I shot him in the chest with our family gun. It was an ancient pistol handed down for a hundred years. A flint lock I believe. In the confusion my son wrestled free. I however took the full brunt of the soldiers' anger. Everything before me disappeared in a profound roar.

I opened my eyes an eternity later. I expected some sort of pain. There was none. I was alone. I wanted to believe everything was fine. Slowly my home came into focus. There it was my home. Alas as I searched I could find no evidence of my children. In my unconsciousness the soldiers must have taken them away. All that was left was a shell of the family I loved so much. The sheer tragedy of it crushed me beyond my deepest thoughts. Again time was still. I was alone. Some one had destroyed my life. My children…I sank into despair.

I do not know how long I pondered the demise of my children. Perhaps it was a moment, or even an eternity. My whole being ached for them. I knew I could never recover. I always said I would die if anything happened to my children. Days came & went. The emptiness of my existence droned on. No one came to see me. It was as if everyone I ever knew ceased to exist. I began to fantasize about each of my children. My favorite one was of Edwardo. He was so strong & handsome. If not for me he would still be alive. I was a horrible mother to let my children die.

In my agony my eyes caught a glimpse of a shadow. It increased in volume each time I glanced away. My depression did not allow for focus so I let it dwindle away. However in the next moment I felt a hand on my shoulder. Surely it was nothing. I shrugged it off as I was now comfortable in my agony. The voice is what got me. It was Edwardo. My shock left me speechless as I caressed his beautiful face. His eyes penetrated my sadness. I felt somewhat alive in my death!

He spoke softly in my ear. He told a most amazing story of a courageous mother who sacrificed herself so that her children would live. This mother now slept in a deep coma hovering between life & death. No one could reach her. No one except a son whose dreams were lucid enough for him to travel to his mother while he slept. His goal was to release her from her self imposed hell. To whisper to her the truth of her last day of life so that she could transcend to a new beginning. Her children all lived.

In his eyes I saw the truth. It was me. I hugged Edwardo for the last time as my son. There would be new roles to play. My children would meet with me again. I lifted my hand over my eyes to shield them from the brilliant sun. Edwardo walked over the ridge to his life. I then turned to my own horizon. What a wonderful son Edwardo was. I noticed others who seemed to appear from nowhere. My coma had finished. I had fulfilled my goal. To protect my children. I was at peace.

Theresa

Oh Was I Mistaken...

Dear friend

Many times in my former life I wished that I was dead. It was mainly a play to relieve the stress I was feeling over various dramas not playing out the way I desired. In retrospect it all seems rather foolish. In my desire not to bore you I will leave out the sordid details of my loudly planned demises. Let's just say that death was a friend that eased the suffering in my soul. I thought it would be the end. Oh was I mistaken...

The last time I declared my death I was standing on a bridge in Vermont. It was a quaint area and instead of enjoying the surroundings I was again brooding about some delusional mishap in my life. I thought that by jumping off the bridge a page would be turned closer to my annihilation. After declaring my intentions I calmed down and decided to wait for another time. Besides I had gotten a lot of attention from my companion that filled me up somehow. Suddenly death lost its appeal. I stepped down from the bridge only to move directly into the path of a drunken driver. He was doing 90 miles an hour.

The impact sent my body sailing into the air. I was conscious but it all seemed like a movie clip in slow motion. My hip hurt a lot and I was wondering how it would feel when I hit the ground. The sky looked ever so blue and my nose felt like it was getting a burn from the sun. Did I wear sunscreen? I had an eternity to ponder over it before I hit. I do not remember if it hurt.

I woke up in a hammock in my mother's back yard. It was still sunny. The screen door slammed and I turned to see my mother bringing out a tray of lemonade. This provoked an avalanche of memory which led me to the realization that my mother had been dead for 10 years. My mom brushed my brow in a familiar loving way that proved to me that it was actually her. Returning her touch it dawned on me that if she were really in front of me then I too was dead. The thought was alarming.

After all my speeches of my desire for death I had finally gotten what I wanted. Here it was a done deal.

My mother welcomed me and gave me the strength to face my new environment. Reluctantly I stepped forward to meet all those who had spent an eternity helping those souls such as myself. It was odd but after all the dramas I had played out about my death I found that I missed life.

Turning back to where I thought the bridge should be I longed to be there again. Physical form is a state not appreciated as well as it should be. Believe me I know.

I have been contemplating my next life and what could be done differently. I am writing to give all of you who desire death a brief look at one who got what she wanted. Life is a cherished gift not to be thrown away on a whim. Nor should it be banished just because it may not be what was planned.

I am ready now to return. This time I will cling to life and honor all it has to offer.

Me

Henry. 1987

Dear friend,

The earth stood still that night I had heard of it happening but ever the skeptic I wrote it off as folly. Surely some over imaginative mind had concocted such a farce to scare young children. There was no such thing. Every sane person knew it. Life was what you held in your hand. There was no more, no less. If there were a God he had long ago forsaken the likes of us and was onto more immediate matters.

The world I knew was filled with tales of the supernatural. All of them not worth a piss if you had asked me. You know what our life was like, scratching out a living the best way we could. We considered ourselves lucky to eat and to have a roof over our heads. There was hardly time to speculate on some foo foo afterlife filled with sacred souls.

Thus I lived my life. I let you pray to our god and respected your need to worship on Sunday. Only did I do so to save friction between us. It was a lot of garbage as far as I was concerned.

That night was different I'll give you that. The storm came up quickly. It was actually a welcome reprieve from the oppressive heat. I was hoping for a nip and a spell on the porch while the wind and the rain washed away the heat. I had just come up the drive when it happened. Your eyes locked to mine in fear. Unable to move neither of us could stop what was about to happen. The lightning struck brutally with pinpoint accuracy. Frozen in the moment I felt a speeding of my blood as it pulsed through my veins. I don't think I uttered a sound although my mouth was wide open.

It didn't hurt. I waited for pain, when it didn't happen I tried to move. The world had slowed down to nothing. Each second was an eternity. My mind raced but my body was moving in slow motion. Your eyes tore into me with such emotion I thought I had been stabbed. Trying to speak or do something, it dawned on me that time was at a standstill. Ironically I found it interesting. I don't know when the exact moment of death came. I didn't feel pain. I had not taken a breath for quite a while. There was a prickly feeling in my hands. I was paralyzed but fully conscious. My whole life began to come alive before me. I saw it all. I began to wonder how long I could stand there while I was dead. I knew it, it just didn't happen like I thought it would. My body was not functioning but I was alive.

My whole belief in life was turned around in that brief eternal moment.

I didn't feel it though I saw my body fall to the ground. I didn't feel any panic, just a curious interest. It was like looking in a mirror although the image did not match. My greatest concern was for you. When my body hit the ground time sped into real time and you were screaming. I tried to stop you from throwing yourself at a body that clearly was not me. You did not listen. You didn't acknowledge my presence. You were obviously hysterical. I had time. I would wait.

The whole process of my death was of little interest to me. In my new state there were constant surprises that kept me intrigued. I waited for you to calm down. I then tried to reason with you that the body you had buried was not me. There were moments when I thought you understood only to be followed by eternal moments of your sorrow. I was at a loss as to what to do.

I left many messages and signs that you did not pick up on. In my frustration I even tried a primitive method of haunting I had seen once in a movie. If there were others surely it was amusing. You did not respond.

I have been dead for nearly a year now. There have been indications that I should move forward and learn more about my surroundings. I cannot however leave you until you hear me. This letter is my last resort. I am trapped in your sorrow. It is my hope you will read this and be assured I am allright.

Henry. 1987

Dear Mother

I know of your sadness and devastation. It permeates my essence. I write so that you may understand. And in that comprehension you may rise above your grief to see the pattern that has unfolded here.

First you must look farther to the whole picture of existence. Each life is but a thread in a fabric of all that is. The interweaving of these threads can be complex. Of course the color scheme should have balance. When you became pregnant with my host there was a great joy. The plans you made were great. But you must realize that however integral you are to my evolution the final choices in my life pattern must be mine. I chose to be born with a short span so that in my living another may continue. Your grief distresses me because I see that you do not understand. The heart I donated to the other child was a karmic ribbon that had to be paid. Rejoice in the knowledge that you helped me in that endeavor.

We will have other opportunities to interact. The child that lives will evolve and help others as I could not have this time. I write so that you will understand. I am able to see a vast variety of dramas. You at this time cannot. This is why I have grasped this moment to tell you. Your soul has asked why...and we have answered. It is not the end of our partnership. There will be another time. Know this.

Me.

All Of Us Here Do Not Regret Dying

Dear friend,

A moment ago or maybe three, I was alive and breathing just as you are now. The transition was quick but somewhat disturbing. We as humans tend to cling to the breath of life. To release the last gasp of air is chilling. The mind panics as it tries to inhale while the lungs remain inert, lifeless and stagnant.

In the first few seconds there is surprise and thoughtfulness as the psyche adjusts to something new. In my experience I grew impatient as the need for air became futile. My mind not comprehending the actualities became entwined in fiction. This fiction enabled me to bypass a total shut down of all my physical thoughts. Ultimately the thought process pushed me through to where I am now. In an effort to help you the reader of this note I must tell you this. Attempt not to cling to the breath. To try to cling will only cause yourself to become tense and thus delay the process. In delaying the process one becomes involved in a drama that blends closely with fear. As we all know fear is an enemy not to be taken lightly. When the realization of death comes upon you, relax. By allowing the process to proceed on a natural basis it becomes easier. The transition is very momentous and a translation literally to a blink of an eye. Child birth is a much more complicated ordeal. This is a walk in the park and can be so literally if you choose. Once you have crossed the line you will wonder why you were so concerned. Just relax, do not fight the process. It is a fight you most likely will not win.

All of us here do not regret dying. It is an evolutionary process. One does live forever, like a flower. The seed produces the vine. The vine a flower. The flower blossoms then vanishes and dies. However the death is rekindled by a new seed which repeats the process all over again. As we do.

Fear not death. It is not an ending. Just a transition.

Me

Anne Marie 1846

Dear friend

It all happened very quickly in retrospect. Though at the time it seemed an eternity. Time lapsed and portrayed itself as a repeating loop which followed me here to this place. It took some moments before I was able to proceed with the process of my new life. Or should I say my real life. My sister Louise was with me that day. I remember my horror as I saw her sail past me on her way to hit a tree. The wagon wheel split on a rut in the road. As usual we were driving the horses at breakneck speed. When it happened the axle began to drag as the wheel broke off. This caused a lurch and a sag. Louise flew past me with great speed. It was no wonder that upon impact she was immediately gone. Since I was holding the reigns my departure from the wagon was a bit slower but not less deadly. I watched the sky fade from view as my ribs exploded inside of me. I never expected to awaken where I did.

My whole life I had read the bible with my family. I had gone to church every Sunday. Never once did I question my Protestant upbringing. My parents were god fearing souls & attempted to pass that on to my sister and my self. Death seemed very far away to us. It was something that happened to the very old. It was a surprise to me that it was so simple. When I opened my eyes I was sitting not far from the wagon. It was though nothing had really happened. The only evidence was the overturned wagon and the missing horses. Looking around the area I notice that everything was as I had left it. I stood up and began to look for Louise. I could not find her. Panic began to set in as my search was in vain. I knew I needed to get to the next town for help. I did not however want to leave my injured sister alone on the prairie as prey for whatever found her. So I walked the perimeter searching for her. Where could she have gone? I was barely able to put one foot in front of the other. How far could she have gotten. After an hour or so I decided to walk into the next town. Not an easy feat as it was at least 5 miles away and I was on foot.

Determined to get help I trudged onward. The over head sun was pounding on my head reminding me that I should have worn a bonnet. I encountered no one on the road. Perhaps a rabbit crossed my path but no others. I walked at least 10 miles and did not encounter the town I was expecting. Perhaps I had miss calculated the distance. The road seemed endless. The sun had traveled farther to the west but I seemingly had made zero progress. It dawned on me that when I noticed something missing like crickets chirping there was suddenly a bunch of crickets. I looked for birds and found the precise species I was thinking of moments later. I felt thirsty when suddenly a lake appeared and I happened to find an abandoned bucket. Alas however I was unable to find a town. I began to despair when the sun began to set. Papa had warned us about being out on the prairie after dark. It was not safe, especially for a young woman alone. I was very scared. Something was wrong but I was unable to discern exactly what it was. Louise was probably scared too. I had no idea what here injuries might be and I was not able to get her help. Discouraged I leaned into a crevasse of a very large maple tree and fell fitfully asleep.

The night passed quickly which was a surprise. I must have hit my head because time was all distorted for me. The new day breathed new hope into my mind and I was walking again. It seemed so wrong not to encounter any one at all. Where was everyone? I should have found help by now. As soon as I thought it there appeared a lone figure approaching some distance ahead. Shielding my eyes from the sun I was able to make out that it was a man. A very weird looking sort dressed in a peculiar fashion. When we were less that 10 feet apart he broke into a beaming smile like he knew me. I definitely had no idea who he was. I immediately began to tell him of my plight and about the loss of my sister. I must have rattled on for quite some time before he spoke. What he told me stopped me cold. It couldn't be. Louise was just a few feet from me only I couldn't see her. She was living at a faster rate of speed. I, in my denial of my transition was moving ever so slowly. I did not need this person to tell me that I was traveling slow. In my irritation I moved away and began to walk again. This man who called himself Peter followed at a distance. He was beginning to annoy me. If he wasn't going to help me then he should just leave me alone. "On the contrary" he said, "I am helping you. You just do not want to be helped. I will travel with you until you are ready". So it was. I trudged onward with Peter in tow. I lost all track of time but I was determined to find help for my sister. Surely she was dead by now, but it didn't matter. I would find help. There came a time when I became very weary of the walking. I wasn't getting anywhere and Peter was ever vigilant in his quest to follow me.

In exasperation I turned to him and blurted out that if he was so smart why didn't he just help me?

Peter with his irritatingly calm manner said "You need only to ask my help and I will". Rolling my eyes to heaven I said, "Okay then help me. I am lost and cannot find my way". Peter reached for my hand and my anger subsided into tears of disbelief. The setting of the endless road melted away into a cloud like room that seemed to twinkle like candle light. There were so many lights. I kept turning in place trying to comprehend what I was seeing. I had never seen so many lights. My sister was at my side smiling. She seemed to appear from nowhere.

In a rush of relief I embraced Louise. I never wanted to let her go again. I checked every inch of her for injuries. There were none. Baffled that she could be unharmed I turned to Peter. His calm manner was more tolerable now. He did not move his lips but I distinctly heard him speak. I was dead, and had been for quite some time. I just could not accept it. Louise was smiling and also speaking without movement. They both had been with me the entire time, waiting for me to ask for help. My irritation with them both subsided into a wave of great love. I was in a new place. I had much to learn. Looking at all the lights I asked Peter where they were coming from. He replied "Each twinkling light is a universe of souls incarnated. They are walking on paths to this very spot. Would you like to wait with Louise & I to help them when they are ready?" I said yes.

Ann Marie 1846

I Can Tell You That Death Is Smooth

Dear friend,

The days counted toward my death were numerous and monotonous. I spent those moments counting the bruises from the needles while wondering if my skin would ever be the same. The discoloration lent itself to my imagination. I fantasized about being reborn as an African. The thought oddly gave me comfort. As the minutes ticked by the discoloration spread in the feeble attempts to keep me alive. I think I could have stood all the efforts if it had not been for the increasing pain. They tried desperately to stop it but the problem ran rampant in my body. Of course the drugs were helpful but they dulled my perception of those final moments. In my greed for a ray of sunshine I compromised the pain by not taking the medication.

It was debatable for those who loved me but since it was my death the medication was withheld. I wanted to experience the process as I had experienced life. That would be with my eyes wide open.

I remember the final morning. I had asked to be moved closer to the window. I wanted to see the sky. With great effort I sat in a chair for my glimpse of the world. I tried to notice each detail as if by this process it would all come with me. You see I loved life. Death was an early visitor. I felt robbed. There was no bitterness but I did not want to die. The religious propaganda of my youth still prevailed with my family. However I was still searching for the path and now it was to end with myself not ready.

I suddenly felt a catch in my chest. It began as tiny sensation and continued as it spread through my chest. I gripped the chair unable to utter a sound. My mind began to race with panic. This was it! Instead of clinging I tried to calm myself. The outside skyline was funnily in my eye line. My breath became shorter & shorter. I wanted to cry out but sill could not.

This continued for quite some time. The sensation subsided and my lungs continued to breathe in & out. The sun was setting when the nurse came to help me back into bed. With her hand at my elbow I found I stood up easily. Feeling rather agile I took a few halting steps to the bed. This wasn't bad. Perhaps I was reaching an epiphany! I crawled into bed quite pleased with myself. Death would have to wait for one more day. As I pulled the covers up I notice the nurse kneeling by my chair. She was helping some other patient I supposed. It then struck me that I was in a private room. How odd. I observed her leaving the room & returning with two doctors. They were really working on that poor guy. I wish they would just get him out. After all this was my room.

A gurney was brought in and they did take him away. I never saw the poor guy's face. I suppose he wandered in here at some point & decided to kick the bucket.

After that flurry of activity the hospital seemed to acquire a peaceful hush. I had no idea at that time what was really happening. I sat in the dark for a long time waiting for the night nurse to bring me my sleeping pill. She never came. One fellow did show up though. A plain little man that I had seen many times in my life. I couldn't place where though. He came to the edge of the bed & smiled. He asked in the softest of voice if I were ready. Not knowing if he meant for the bed pan or pills I was confused.

Smiling he told me that I should come with him. Didn't he realize I was waiting to die? The face that reflected me spoke again with this line. "You have".

I can tell you now that death is smooth. You may wait for it, defy it, run from it, or face it with your eyes open. It comes silently and the result is wondrous. It continues in circular fashion back to life. Life in several specific ways. Some you know others you do not.

I find myself now toying with the second half of this circle. I see the sunrise in the distance. I am on my way. You know African American this round would be an interesting choice.

Me.

Asaka

dear friends

one wonders frequently why we exist. there are
many thoughts also as to why we die. the thoughts
attached to the process are always filled with questions.
i too was wondering.   i spent countless hours in
contemplation during my lifetime. no answers ever
availed me. disappointed at the end i continued to
question even after the life. surely i was astounded at
what i found upon arrival. no thoughts in life ever
prepare one for the moment of transition. no words to
describe the events as they unfold. each experience has
terrific individuality.   this is the reason for all the
speculation while living.

if i had a nickel for every word written about death
by the living i would have been a wealthy man. the
living never fully remembering, always tend to confuse.
thus the uniqueness of thoughts from a "dead man", one
who in the moment can clarify exactly what is there.

let me introduce the one who is i, my name is
irrelevant but for stability i choose asaka. egyptian in
origin, one of my most favorite existences. the summer
sky of night always enthralling. the possibilities of life

displayed in multidimensional visions. gaze at the night sky that is a good display of death and its possibilities. endless. each light a moment for memory. each black void holding promise of possibilities as a blank canvass awaiting an artist. the best advice, become an artist. add color to the nothingness. it is good to practice as a living soul. in death the possibilities increase. the practice making the next moment more exciting. look to the living moments as a training ground. you become your actions. those actions translate in death to your canvass. belief is irrelevant. all is as i have told you. i am here. the body is gone but i see through the eyes of my soul. the vision is clear. embrace the moment.

Asaka

dear friends

    one wonders frequently why we exist. There are many thoughts also
as to why we die. the thoughts attached to the process are always filled
with questions. I too was wondering. i spent countless hours in comtemplation
during my lifetime. no answers ever availed me. disappointed at the end
i continued to question even after the life. surely i was asbunded at what i
found upon arrival. no thoughts in life ever prepare one for the moment of
transition. no words to describe the events as they unfold. each experience
has terrific individuality. this is the reason for all the speculation
while living

    If i had a nickel for every word written about death by the living.
I would have been a wealthy man. the living never fully remembering.
always tend to confuse. Thus the uniqueness of thoughts from a "dead
man", one who in the moment can clarify exactly what is there

    . let me introduce the one who is i, my name irrelevant but for stability
i choose asaka. eygptian in origin. one of my most favorite existances.
the summer sky of night always enthralling. the possibilities of
life display in multidimensial visions. gaze at a night sky. that
is a good display of death and its possibilities. endless. each light
a moment for memory. each black void holding a promise of possibalte
as a blank canvass awaiting an artist. the best advice. become an
artist. add color to the nothingness. it is good to practice as living
soul. in death the possibilites increase. the practice making the next
moment more exciting. look to the living moments as a training ground.
you become your actions. those actions translate in death to your
canvass. belief is irrelivant. all is a ___ i have told you. i am here.
the body is gone but i see through the eyes of my soul. the vision
is clear. embrace the moment

Asaka

Mary Pat Stein 1899

Dear friend

As I look back upon the body I so cherished, laughter spills from me. The hysterical outburst borne of fear does nothing to clam the panic building inside me. The mere thought that there is not longer an inside of me sends tremors though me. Why should I be frightened? There is no longer any reason to fear for my safety. My well toned body lies inert at my feet. The blood vessels collapsing, the heart ceasing to beat. The attachment for it begins to wane slightly. I reach out to touch the soft skin and to wipe a stray strand of hair from my brow. Such a fragile thing this body. A wonder it lasted as long as it did. How strange now to view the self I thought was me. With out my essence to fill it the resemblance fades. I laughed again to think how attached I was. This body in no way represents who I am. It was merely a costume donned for an experience. An experience now complete.

I use to be worried that my individuality would not survive death. That somehow "I" would be sucked into an eternal void never to remember who I was.

Now the realization of the thousand me's represented in my essence all live on. I was so much more than Mary Pat Stein. I could list all the names but that is not my reason for writing. The remembrance of who I was in this body will remain with me for an eternity just like all the other lives. I use this vehicle for telling my tale for those of you with the same questions as I.

I hope you understand. If not now perhaps when you gaze back upon your own inert body.

Mary Pat Stein 1899

Dear friend

As I look back upon the body I so cherished, laughter spills from me. The hysterical outburst borne of fear does nothing to calm the panic building inside me. The mere thought that there is no longer an inside of me sends tremors through me. Why should I be frightened? There is no longer any reason to fear for my safety. My well toned body lies inert at my feet.

. . .

I was so much more than Mary Pat Stein. I could list all the names but that is not my reason for writing. The remembrance of who I was in this body will remain with me for an eternity just like all the other lives. I use this vehicle for telling my tale for those of you with the same questions as I. I hope you understand. If not now perhaps when you gaze back upon your own inert body.

Mary Pat Stein
1899

107

Lizette

Dear Allen

C'est moi! I have maneuvered myself to this moment to bid you Bonjour. Do you not remember me? If you cannot guess I will tell you. Lizette as you know moi. This thing you do with your wife is so beneficial. It is a rebirth and finish for those living and not in the physical. My correspondence with you previously prepared me immensely for my transition. No one understood when I recounted my dreams and said that gave me comfort. They were sure the fever had made me mad! I was never sure myself until I opened my spiritual eyes. Physical life is like a multifaceted bead. It is one but each side bears a different reflection. Together these reflections offer a twinkling beam of light to guide one to the real life. It was important that we met. The proof to young souls incarnated or merely the suggestion of truth that there is more than one path is large. Much larger than you or I ever thought when our paths crossed. Forever grateful am I for the encounter.

I await incarnation. There are many souls in need of a voice. A voice to resound the truth. We know that truth it is up to us to live it. Thus I wait till the moment is right.

One would suppose that there are many stars in the sky. What if each was a reflection of one's inner possibilities. You taught me anything is possible. For that I thank you. The opportunity to communicate was too fresh to pass up.

We will meet again. I am proud of your progress. Do you still have a box of winter in your house?

Lizette.

(Note: The "box of winter" refers to a refrigerator, something that Lizette found in an earlier visit where she walked around a friend's apartment while using the medium's body.)

Dear Allen

C'est moi! I have maneuvered myself to this moment to bid you Bonjour. Do you not remember me. If you cannot guess I will tell you. Lizette as you know moi. This thing you do with your wife is so beneficial. It is a rebirth and finish for those living and not in the physical. My

...

is possible. For that I thank you. The opportunity to communicate was too fresh to pass up.

We will meet again. I am proud of your progress.

Do you still have a box of winter in your house?

Lizette

Edward

Dear friend

T'was another day of cold and rain. Always filled with dread and hunger I struggled to stand in me mother's stone kitchen. My bones felt brittle. Like in any moment they would splinter away and I'd be left in a heap on the floor. There was but a bit of tea and some stale loaf heels. Not much to fill one's belly but something all the same. On a better day I would have gathered meself down to the school yard to be learning my ABC's. Learning so important to me parents. I saw no worth in it but went all the same to save my poor mother's heart.

On this day however I stayed home close to the hearth. There had been a few days of fever. Not as high as Tess Mulcarrey's but a fever all the same. Some said her nose bled for 2 days and nights. Some say she's about to die. I checked me sleeve each time my nose drips for drops of blood. None so far but the ache in my limbs is almost unbearable. I stick my bare feet closer to the fire but it only seems to get worse. Mother wipes my brow and prays to the Virgin Mary. It's all she can do. I remember closing my eyes while

111

sipping the last of the tea. Its warmth suddenly increasing inside my belly. A burning right through my insides. Like I was on fire. I heard me mother calling my name but the warmth felt so good to my weary bones. I decided to answer her later. I suddenly heard no more.

The ache in my knees was gone. It seemed I slept for days. Tossing and turning I opened my eyes to find meself in a lovely feather bed. It scared me for though I had heard they existed I had never seen one.

There was no sign of my mother or the hearth. This place seemed like a dream. Whatever it was I felt fine. Fine as compared to the gates of misery. The pain no longer my companion I found myself assessing my surroundings. This was an image of my home but a richer version. All was well with my body. Hunger not an issue. Surely I had died and went to heaven.

I called for me mother. She never answered. In a panic I began to call loudly. No one came. Desperately I ran to the hearth. In the flames I could see my mother. She was washing a child's body. She was crying and crying to the Virgin Mary. In a moment I realized she was preparing me for my burial. Indeed I had died. So odd a feeling. Knowing that one is dead. Yet continuing to be concerned about it all. Thoughts coming into my head now. Like little voices, whispers of knowledge that kept increasing.

I wanted to comfort my mother but knew that she would suffer my death regardless. My destiny now unfolding. It does not include going back there. I close my eyes and feel a rush of spirit. Hard to describe to those still physical. I must go now the vast horizon awaits me.

Edward

Jeffrey

Dear friend

I know how you cling to life. The idea that it will cease to be is hard for the mind to comprehend. The memory of other times somehow never comes to mind until after the deed is done. Hardly comforting in the moment.

I know you mourned my untimely death. The sense of your sorrow reached me. However trapped in the moment of revelation I was unable to communicate with you as we had planned in our youth. The lack of contact most likely set you into a spiral of disappointment because if there were life I surely would have kept my word and let you know.

The initial revelation is spell binding and the perception of time totally diminished. To you it's been a long time. For myself a brief interlude. Non physical existence is difficult if not impossible to describe to physical beings. Even with my blue blood education the vocabulary does not exist.

Upon my acclimation my thought was to contact you. Immediately you presented yourself to me. It was the communication problem that I did not count on.

Laughing I tried the tricks we saw in movies about poltergeists and the like. None of them ever worked. In disappointment I followed you hoping for a brief moment of clarity between us. My only opportunity has presented itself in the person who writes for those who cannot. My only hope is that you find this. Acceptance is critical in this endeavor. If I don't get another opportunity, know this. I will wait at the door for you. I will not tarry in other dimensions like we spoke of. I will be there to guide you. In my arms you will have no fear. The time is coming. You know that too. Perhaps my death was not so untimely after all.

I am here. We will be together.

Jeffrey

Dear friend

I know how you cling to life. The idea that it will cease to be is hard for the mind to comprehend. The memory of other times somehow never comes to mind until after the deed is done. Hardly comforting in the moment.

...

I will be there to guide you. You will have no fear. The time is coming. You know that too. Perhaps my death was not so untimely after all.

I am here. We will be together

Jeffrey

Raymond

Dear Friend

MY WORST FEAR VISITED ME FOR THE LAST TIME LAST NIGHT. THE LAST EXHALE OF BREATH LEFT MY LUNGS AND I ENTERED THE VOID THAT HAD LEFT ME COLD IN LIFE. I ALWAYS WONDERED WHAT WOULD REALLY HAPPEN IN THE FIRST SECOND AFTERWARDS. WOULD I BE AWARE? WOULD I PANIC, WOULD I BE IN PAIN? THE WHOLE THING HAD NEVER BEEN TRANSLATED REALISTICALLY BY ANYONE WITH THE EXCEPTION OF RELIGIOUS ORDERS. SO I WAS AFRAID, TERRIBLY AFRAID. NOW IN RETROSPECT I SEE DIFFERENTLY. IF SOMEONE HAD ONLY TOLD ME IT WOULD HAVE BEEN DIFFERENT. THUS MY REASON FOR WRITING.

THIS CONNECTION IS FAULTY SO I WILL CONTINUE WITHOUT FURTHER ADIEU.

I HAD CANCER. THE BAD KIND BROUGHT ON BY UNRESOLVED ISSUES. IT WAS INTENSIFIED BY MY FEAR OF THE FIRST MOMENT OF DEATH. PERHAPS MY LIFE WOULD HAVE BEEN PROLONGED IF I HAD KEPT MY FOCUS ELSEWHERE. EVERY AVENUE OF TREATMENT WAS EXPLORED. I PUT UP A PRETTY GOOD FIGHT HOWEVER

117

EACH MOMENT WAS LEADING ME TO THE MOMENT I DREADED.

THEY SENT ME HOME FROM THE HOSPITAL TO DIE. TOO BAD THE DEMONS CAME WITH ME. THEY HAUNTED MY DREAMS SHOWING ME GRISLY VISIONS OF WHAT WAS TO COME. I BECAME PARALYZED WITH ANTICIPATION. MY MIND BECAME DIVIDED AGAINST ITSELF. ONE SIDE WANTED TO LIVE AS LONG AS POSSIBLE, THE OTHER JUST WANTED IT OVER.

THAT LAST NIGHT AS I LABORED TO KEEP MY BODY ALIVE I REALIZED THAT THE MOMENT HAD COME. I ALMOST THREW UP WITH THE THOUGHT.

I WAS IN MY BED. ALL OF MY FAMILIAR OBJECTS ABOUT ME. I KEPT MY EYES OPEN AND BEGAN TO COUNT HOW LONG IT TOOK TO INHALE & EXHALE. AFTER A BIT IT BECAME INCREASINGLY DIFFICULT TO INHALE. GREEDY FOR ONE MORE MOMENT OF LIFE I HELD MY BREATH. I FELT THE DEFLATION AS I LET IT OUT. SUDDENLY I KNEW I WOULD NOT INHALE AGAIN. AND YOU KNOW NOTHING CHANGED. THE ROOM REMAINED. I SUDDENLY FELT LIKE AN ICE CREAM CONE. I GOT UP OUT OF BED AND WENT TO THE KITCHEN. I HAD NOT BEEN UP IN QUITE A WHILE. AS I REACHED IN THE FREEZER I REALIZED THAT THIS WAS THE MOMENT I HAD

DREADED MY WHOLE LIFE. AND HERE I WAS EATING ICE CREAM.

I WANTED TO LAUGH. THEN I WANTED TO CRY. I SETTLED ON FINISHING THE ICE CREAM.

I WALKED BACK TO MY BED. THERE I WAS LOOKING QUITE PEACEFUL. I DID NOT LINGER LONG. THERE WAS SO MUCH TO SEE. MY SURROUNDINGS WERE TRANSPOSING TO ANOTHER PLACE. THIS ABILITY WAS VERY EXCITING. SO MUCH MORE THAN PHYSICAL.

I AM HAPPY, MY FEAR WAS UNFOUNDED. BUT I WOULD HAVE WRITTEN TO YOU WHOEVER YOU ARE. FUNNY HOW THESE THINGS WORK OUT. HOPE IT SOOTHS THE FEAR IN YOU.

RAYMOND

DEAR FRIEND

MY WORST FEAR VISITED ME FOR THE LAST TIME LAST NIGHT. THE LAST EXHALE OF BREATH LEFT MY LUNGS AND I ENTERED THE VOID THAT HAD LEFT ME COLD IN LIFE. I ALWAYS WONDERED WHAT WOULD REALLY HAPPEN IN THE FIRST SECOND AFTERWARDS. WOULD I BE AWARE? WOULD I PANIC, WOULD I BE IN PAIN? THE WHOLE THING HAD NEVER BEEN TRANSLATED REALISTICALLY BY ....

Eddie

Dear friend

I never expected to have this opportunity. Now that it has arrived I am filled with anxiety in hopes I can convey my message properly. Anyone connected with my life has long since passed to where I am now. Forgiveness for trespasses have long been achieved. This note is for those still in the physical anticipating violence. An odd thought coming from one who should be removed from such blatantly physical acts. After all once life is over you get another chance to rectify errors. Right? It ain't always so. In fact dark deeds follow you where ever you go. Let me tell you how it was for me.

I grew up in the Bronx at the beginning of the century that you know as 1900. I lived in a walkup off of Columbus Ave. Pretty shabby but clean I was one of eleven children. Now you can imagine the competition just to eat. I learned very young that a con was always worth it if worked properly. I quit school at age of 12. What was the use? Where was I gonna go? I could read + do numbers, what else was there. I started running errands for a neighborhood boss when I was

14. My old man was actually pleased. I was just one less mouth at the dinner table.

I spent my teen years learning from the best Micky the Masher, Ready Robert and Felix. By the time I was eighteen I carried a gun and wore a new suit and I sure didn't have to worry 'bout eatin'. I had plenty of dames, booze, food you name it. I only had to do one thing. Kill people.

The first time I wasted someone I went home + threw up. These two cons were tryin to run numbers and it was getten in Mickey's face. So I was told to warn em + then take care of em. It got easier + easier as the years went by. I lived the good life. My children were not hungry.

It happened when I was having dinner at Prolovones. On minute I'm sippin' wine the next sippin' blood. It happened so fast that I didn't get a chance to even get up. I remember hearing my heart beat soundly in my ears. Everything else was a blur. Only my heart beat was clear. I felt sad as it went slower + slow. Finally there was silence and I felt worse.

I woke up in what I first thought was a hospital. I soon realized that it wasn't. So okay I'm in hell or maybe if I played it right to the Pearly Gates. Where the hell was St. Pete?

Beings that I couldn't really understand came into the room. I was asked what I wanted to do? I could re enter the physical or I could atone there. I wasn't sure what the atone business was but I was sure I didn't want to go back to physical. Had enough of that thank you.

I was told that because of all the violence I had perpetrated in the universe that I must be the one to return balance. Well if it meant the Pearly Gates sure. I sat in a chair in the middle of nowhere. I mean there simply wasn't nothing there. Then like a huge movie screen the film started playing. Or maybe not a film. Anyways the next thing I know I'm seeing all the people I blew away. In a very weird moment I felt all of their pain and the pain of all those who loved them. It was horrifying. I screamed for mercy. I screamed for it to stop and was told that I was the creator of it all. I screamed for a chance to fix it and was told that I was in that moment given the chance.

Let me say at the end I understood the folly of my deeds. Whatever you put out there relives itself in you forever. So if you're contemplating evil in any form,

think again.   Your creations are you.   And you will
have to walk through your gallery when you die.

I hope someone reads this for I am still creating the
balance. Take it from a dead man. This isn't a joke.

Eddie

Dear friend
I never expected to have this opportunity. Now that it has
arrived I am filled with anxiety in hopes I can convey
my message properly. Anyone connected with my life has
long since passed to where I am now. Forgiveness for

...

evil in any form. Think again. Your creations are you.
and you will have to walk through your
gallery when you die.
I hope someone reads this for I am still
creating the balance. Take it from a dead man.
this isn't a joke.

Eddie

Dear friend,

As I sit and ponder the meaning of life I chuckle at the irony of it all. Now I can see the multitude of choices my essence has made

...

your spirited eyes. There will be rejoicing. Do not fear death. That is our message to you

T. Mary

T Mary

Dear friend,

As I sit and ponder the meaning of life I chuckle at the irony of it all. Now I can see the multitude of choices my essence has made many many times. I cling to my last life because it is the one closest to me in this moment. However even if I chose to believe that that personality was the totality of me, I was wrong. It used to scare me that my death would bring about annihilation. That the "me" I cherished would be lost forever upon that last breath. I spent too much time wrapped up in that thought. I allowed the fear to fill me and thus my death was more difficult than it needed to be. I was so surprised when all of my lives reunited upon my passing. Instead of annihilation there was rejuvenation. The physical body so un <u>necessary</u> to real life. I feel free and full of new thoughts + discoveries. It is not clear to me yet whether I will choose to be physical yet. The importance of it escapes me upon blending with the others.

You wonder why we write? We do for the reassurance to you that there is more. It is not like anything you could imagine right now. You will remember when you open your spiritual eyes. There will be rejoicing. Do not fear death. That is our message to you.

T Mary

Arthur

Dear Friend

The first thing I noticed was the absence of breath. My lungs laboring to intake air through the ventilator. I could hardly remember what it was like to be free of the blasted thing. Too many cigarettes, clogging my breathing. Often I was asked why I kept doing it. I had no idea other than I liked the way the smoke filtered through my body. The debt was paid in my last year of life. I spent 427 days hooked up to the machine that kept me breathing. It was said it wasn't noisy but it reverberated in my ears. The silence greeted me one morning followed by a brief suspicion that something was up. I looked around my room but nothing was out of place. Just a silence. I hadn't been up for a while so I rang for a nurse. No one showed. It was if there had been an evacuation without my knowledge.

I figured someone would show sooner or later so I drifted back on my pillow and dozed. I started to think about when I first moved to New York after college. One of my best memories was having a cigarette + martini at the Tavern on the Green. It was a celebration of sorts on getting my first job. It was then I heard a noise. Abruptly my eyes opened and I found my self sitting at a table at the Tavern on the Green. A glass tinkled and the gentle murmur of the lunch crowd flooded my senses. Was it a dream? Surely not. I stood up and went to the door trying to make sense of what was happening. Every detail was exactly as I remembered it. I rubbed my eyes and thought of my childhood when my brother had played a stupid trick on me in the second grade. He rearranged our room so that everything was backward just to spook me. I rubbed my eyes again and there I was in my old room, rearranged just like he had done. This process continued until I was sure I was mad.

After a while I covered my eyes to stop the transitions. It was like being on a roller coaster and it was making my stomach woozy. I felt a hand on my shoulder but I was afraid to look up. There was a gentle voice that sounded familiar. I was told that I could control what was happening. Thought creates reality and I was running rampant through the process. All I had to do was slow down. Think slowly. I could be anywhere I wanted from now on. The truth of it was that I was dead.

Funny. I wasn't upset. I opened my eyes and looked immediately into my brother's eyes. I had not seen them for so very long.

The sound of breathing no longer necessary a dim memory I am too busy creating realities with my brother. Death is only the beginning. I am having fun. You will too.

Arthur

Sebastian

Dear friend

I was with you but a brief moment. The measurement of time dims in my memory. But I can recall the quantity of it. The quantity was small but completely exhilarating. I wanted to experience your touch once again. The smooth skin of your palm on my cheek is a memory I've carried from life to life. When the opportunity arose to be your child I was unable to say no. Now sensing your grief I feel perhaps it was a selfish error. Your guilt also disturbs me. My demise was of my own lack of decision. The sights + sounds of physical life enveloped me from the first breath. I was intoxicated with the denseness of it all. Waiting to develop all of my senses was trying to say the least. The small burst of temper you never understood was merely my frustration at the physical limitations. The measurement of time was excruciatingly slow. When I was finally able to walk it was no wonder I took off in such haste. I wanted to feel the wind whistle by my ears. I wanted to taste the air as I was breathing. I wanted to look into the blue sky and immerse my self in the color.

I wanted to feel the grass press against my back. All these things I did feel when I ran from you that morning. In complete abandon without any caution I stepped in front of that bicycle. It shouldn't have killed me but my skull had not completely developed and the damage was severe. It was a moment however of complete joy for me. I was able to consume the whole experience in an instant. My only regret is your sadness. Please do not feel badly. The experience was in line with my growth. Know that by my lack of perception I was killed, not by anything you did or didn't do.

Know that I still exist and that you will experience my essence again. Perhaps in a different format. I understand your isolation but you are choosing to put yourself there. This experience has benefited us both. I can't say I'll wait for you but know that our essences are drawn to each other. The magnetism will occur again.

Be at peace. Know no guilt. It was my choice. Stand up and live this life you have taken. It's the only way to reunion.

I love you.
Sebastian

Francois 1749

Dear Friend

I was so afraid. It enveloped me like a glove clinging to every curve of my physical being. My thoughts became muddled as the progression of events unfolded. The stories told in Sunday school were not complete. The fear of change never addressed. The physical transitions never classified so that one may know what to expect. I appreciate the opportunity to share my experience. Hope prevails in my essence with the knowledge someone may benefit from my experience.

I knew I was ill. I could feel it in my fingertips. Still I ignored all the signs in hope that it would just diminish. There was an inkling that I was the creator, only I did not understand the seed that started it all. Once a life begins it is difficult to turn the tide. Still I knew. The tingling was evident from the start. In my denial the disease progressed rapidly until all hope of recovery faded. It was sad but inevitable. My last week was not revealed to me as such. A blessing to be sure. If I had realized it was my last morning it would have been more difficult. I felt a rattle in the morning -

133

something like an empty jar. It passed as the sun moved across the sky. I remember looking out at the garden and making a note to plant new flowers. I did not know that that would be impossible. The grip of the first seizure came swiftly. I fell against the kitchen counter quite perplexed at the abruptness of it. I managed to get to the couch before my legs gave out. A shocking experience to loose control over one's body. As each part of me gave way to the end, I became less fearful. Suddenly the process seemed safe. I knew that the "me" inside would be around after the body I knew as "me" faded away.

The last breath was difficult as mentally I knew it was the last. I so liked breathing. It was surprising to be functional while being un-functional. Sort of a contradiction. There was no pain. Just an easing of breath. And once it was gone I wondered of its necessity at all. There is so much here. Everything one can think of! The predictions were clear + true. We can create anything we desire. The pain is gone, merely a reflection of my issues. Now I am perceiving how to resolve them. It is an interesting process.

All is so clear. All is well. Do not be afraid. It's everything + it is nothing. Something to ponder. If you like we will await you.

adieu

Francois

1749

135

Sanford

Dear friend

How astounding death is! To suddenly see the path one has taken and all of its incriminations. The veil of reason lifted until the obvious confronts you so bluntly. It was so with I. The final moments anticipating the unknown. Fearful yet exhilarating in a perverse sort of way. The last breath escaping through soulful fingertips. The precise moment of physical collapse enduring yet so final. Let me tell you, a feeling of triumph. Yes triumph over the physical machinations. To know that one continues after the final moment. So exhilarated was I. However the becoming of spiritual again is no simple task. Gone are the physical masquerades one becomes so accustomed to. In death there are no masquerades. One might wish it but that will only last as long as the last pump of blood through failing tissues. Once eyes are dead the true reality manifests itself and all bets are off.

Such as it was for me.

I lived a life of promise hiding behind truth. The truth being I beheld no promise. Each moment blending into the next in a flurry of half truths and stage dramas. So caught up in the script I ceased to be myself and became a star player in an un fulfilling drama. Of course I never realized this until later. In my last moments the realization materialized and bombarded me upon separation from the physical. My best advice is to be yourself. No matter how un endearing to others it may seem. To be hiding behind a mask only does dis service to yourself. Belief is not necessary. Your truth will reveal itself and there will be no argument with what is written. Until then live to the fullest.

Sanford

Dear friend

A chance to do something noble usually
comes around only a few times in ones life. For
myself it came several however I missed all
my chances. Caught up in a self indulgent life
style I let opportunity slip through my fingers.
By that I mean the opportunity to help others.

. . .

. . .

When your moment arrives perhaps you will
remember this letter. Perhaps it will ease
your anxiety. Perhaps I will be there to meet
you. Perhaps we will connect and be friends
It is my hope.

Sincerely
Anton

Anton

Dear friend

A chance to do something noble usually comes around only a few times in one's life. For myself it came several however I missed all my chances. Caught up in a self indulgent life style I let opportunity slip through my fingers. By that I mean the opportunity to help others. My focus so blurred by my own ambition. I thought I was making great choices. Now it seems I did not.

My death was swift. Accidents usually are. Although now I pause when calling these incidents accidents. They are simply a rendezvous with our self created destiny. I had been on the path to mine for years. The details would bore the reader and are not necessary to the point of this communication. Death is but a facilitator to allow you to reach your home. Life as one knows it does not really exist in that way. The rumors of its illusions are somewhat true. The dramas created to distract one from the real focus of existence. In retrospect I see the truth. It would have made a difference had I realized it while physical.

Now after retrospection I have been gifted with a second opportunity. The ability to communicate placed before me like a jewel. Do I hoard it? Do I hide it away in fear that someone will take it from me? Do I flash its importance as a medal of distinction for myself? All of these thoughts have passed through my mind. Yet I am driven to share them with you. It is the noble thing to do. My continued existence serves as a beacon of hope to all those fearful of annihilation through death. It simply is not so. I am proof. You may disregard me. Indeed I hope not. I cannot offer validity other than my own testament. I watched my funeral. I felt the life force leave my body and continued. I was the life force not my physical form.

When your moment arrives perhaps you will remember this letter. Perhaps it will ease your anxiety. Perhaps I will be there to meet you. Perhaps we will connect and be friends. It is my hope.

Sincerely

Anton

Nathaniel

Dear friend

Deep within the murky sea does my body rest. Preserved like a mummy beneath the glass tomb. The others surround me like a dinner for eight. No reservations needed there's plenty of seating for all. Excuse my mirth at such dire straits but I'm not really there at all. I remember the moment, the last gasp of air as my ship sank down to the bottom. Being the captain I was to go down with my lady. Alas in the final seconds my bravo escaped me and I clamored for the sky as well. The rush of the sea came swiftly. My thought to hold my breath until another opportunity to breathe presented itself. It was not to be. The one fine window imported directly from France loosened itself in my hands. Its weight bore down on my soddened body. Pushing me down down down til I hit the bottom. The glass offered a crystal view of all coming down to their deaths. I watched much longer than I was breathing to be sure. Not a body survived the deadly ship however all the souls lived on.

As close to the sea as we all were it was difficult to move on you know. So we stayed a lot longer than we should have. Til the flesh fell from our old bones. Under water development so fascinating to a lover of the sea.

We all know it's time to move on. We stopped counting the moments long ago. We understand there is a place to go where we can request a sea life again. There are these souls who come to us to see if we are ready to go.

I write this note before I leave. I hope you whoever you are gets it. It's just an observation. Mine of course. I just thought someone ought to know.

Nathaniel

Dear friend

Deep within the murky sea does my body rest. Preserved like a mummy beneath the glass tomb. The others surround me like a dinner for eight. No reservations needed there's plenty of seating for all. Excuse my mirth at such dire straits but I'm not really there at all. I remember the moment, the last gasp of air as my ship sank down to the bottom. Being the captain I was to go down with my lady. Alas in the final seconds my brain escaped me and

...

I write this note before I leave, I hope you whoever you are gets it. It's just an observation Mine of course. I just thought someone ought to know.

Nathan

143

Seemo

Dear friend

No matter how many times I die I somehow manage to be buried in snow. Upon wakening into spiritual I look back in amusement at my demise. It puzzles me that I cannot remember something about each of those deaths where I could possibly step back in time to save myself.

I know I have never feared death while physical. The likelihood of a painful one never crossing my mind. The process relatively routine has become like an epic to me. Each life a new chapter in my ever evolving adventure. I guess one would term me as an old soul. In this moment I cannot give you details of past existences. I can however remember the lesson themes of all of them. It's difficult to describe my exact whereabouts at the moment. My thoughts swirl before me in a constant changing pattern. I'm sure you've heard the adage "Thought creates reality". It is even more true when you are dead. Your thoughts project immediately within you and the experience is immediate.

Death should not be described as an ending. It's thought provoking but so untrue. It is merely an adapting to a new set of surroundings. My only desire in this communication is to share my awareness of what a simple process it is.

I am curious by my repeated endings buried deep in snow. The guides smile patiently as I try to make sense of it. Surely there is no karmic energy attached. Perhaps it is just a coincidence. Yeah right.

I leave you now to ponder my strange rambling. Hopefully it will provoke you to think further about your own death. It is inevitable but not an abrupt stop.

I leave you to your thoughts.

Seemo

Hector: "We Are But A Breath Apart"

Dear Friend

I trace the outline of your face with my spirit finger tips. Surely you feel the energy as it escapes. Wrapped in a blanket you lament my death. I turn to smoke in hopes of permeating your being so that you may know I am here. Existence has many layers. We are but a breath apart. My electric energy pattern varies from yours in this dimension. My consummate desire is to communicate with you. To comfort you in your moment of loss. I am not lost merely transformed. You too shall emerge as a spiritual being when your physical shell is no more. I cannot await your arrival as I continue to evolve. This evolution does not separate us. It is a physical illusion. In my state of existence I will always be able to be with you. My only wish in this moment is to be physical for one brief moment to be able to wipe the tears from your cheeks.

Attempt to connect with the energy of life. Give of yourself to the comfort of others. Through this you will be able to find me. I exist through divine energy now. I continue to evolve. My heart is filled with love for you.

Move forward to the light. I am there and ever shall be. I cannot wait but will transfer myself to you. Fear not the ending of this particular phase. Cry not for me. If you must cry then you cry for yourself and then move through the self pity. You must retain the energy level that connected us in the first place. To be in doom will only divide us further. I wipe the tears from your cheeks. Your eyes flutter briefly and then you sleep. Still beautiful I am in awe of your presence. I love you. Please heed my advice.

Hector

Dear Friend

I trace the outline of your face with my spirit finger tips. Surely you feel the energy as it escapes. Wrapped in a blanket you lament my death I turn to smoke in hopes of permeating your being so that you may know I am here. Existance has many layers. We are but a breath apart. My electric energy pattern varies from yours in this dimension. My consumate desire is to communicate with you. To comfort you in your moment of loss. I am not lost merely transformed. You too shall emerge ... when your physical shell is no more.

...

Please heed my advice

Hector

Jeremy

Dear friend

I did not want to die. It was so unfair! Just when my life was starting to make sense! I clung to every breath hoping for a miracle. The sound of air as it escaped my nostrils gave me comfort, especially at the end. With each intake of air I purposely exhaled...just one more time. An act of defiance for one so close to the surrender. I was dying from deep within. My blood betraying my cells with toxins. It was all so unjust. I stopped praying. What God would permit such a thing. I was angry. God was an easy target. I needed to blame someone or something.

So I waited for death to over take me. I expected to just black out. I expected there to be a God so I could tell him off. I expected more panic with the last breath. I expected all these things but did not get any.

On the dawn of the day, the pain was becoming unbearable. Until now I had declined any pain killers. I wanted to remain whole in my head. I feared drugs but on this last day I decided to ease the burden.

When the morphine hit my head began to spin a web of lies. It told my body there was no pain. And my body believed it. Closing my eyes I entered a zone of silence. It echoed off the chambers of my mind. I soon began to run thoughts of my life experiences. I remembered childhood antidotes, school plays, and family episodes. I felt my body relax as I relived old memories. It was better.

My uncle Victor took me horseback riding. We were riding on a beach when it struck me that it never would have happened in this way. I had grown up in Oklahoma. There were no beaches. I caught up with my uncle, who was staring out at the horizon. I asked him why my memories were inaccurate. He told me that we had ridden together many times in this fashion. I knew that even in my morphine haze that there had never been a beach. Uncle Vic looked me in the eye and smiled. "Wouldn't you have wished it to be true? Now you can have the experience any way you like." I was stunned. Did this mean what exactly. Uncle Vic continued to smile. He turned in his saddle and said "Well you can ride back to where you came from or you can ride with me towards the sun. Of if you like we can make it a moon." I repeated my preference to live. Death was so final and I had so much to live for. With that Uncle Vic began to chuckle again. He told me that I was confused about the living part. He said that life evolves constantly. I was merely shedding some skin and that the next phase of life was just as great. "Come on" he said. "Ride with me just a little while. You'll start to see what I mean." I loosened my grip on the reins and followed. Each step my horse took felt lighter and lighter. When we reached the horizon I looked back and saw to my surprise the edges of my old life. It somehow looked smaller and less significant from this perspective. And there were no beaches to ride on. I decided to follow Uncle Vic. That's when I realized Uncle Vic had died when I was a teenager. I guess he did know the beach better than I.

So I let go of my obsession with that particular life. There were many more on the horizon. I'll get to them. For now I'll just follow the coastline with Uncle Vic. It's a great way to live, from any perspective.

Jeremy

Jerry 99

Dear friend

What I miss most about physical reality is the wind. Its random gusts of energy that cause various movements in the way of things. Following my death there was a prolonged moment of stillness that lingers even now. My guess at the time was that the quiet was necessary to my realization of the life I had just lived.

According to my memory it was rather nondescript. I probably made choices in haste on that one in my haste to reincarnate. You are most likely not interested so much in my previous life but more so about where I am now.

Let me tell you it's not what the fables spoke of. I use the word fable as it gives the picture of something contrived for the so called good of the populace. Between you and I, my preference would have been for the old fashioned truth between the eyes. Enough of this rubbish about heaven + hell. Catechism classes painted a rather distorted picture of the way things go here. The direction of the well intentioned truly muddles up one's perspective. It took some effort on my part to separate what I expected from what really was.

I could ramble on about my expectations but would rather move toward the way of things here.

The ability to direct thought supercedes anything you can think of on the earth plane. Manifestation quadruples in strength. I guess the level of intensity was always there just not realized until arrival here. I was bumbling about trying to make sense of my demise. At first I was not very pleased with death's outcome.

My expectations of pearly gates got in the way somewhat. There are not any gates, only the trappings of my mind.

I am still adjusting but I will tell you it is better here. I miss the wind but welcome the ability to manifest. With practice the wind will return. You see I've only been here a day and a night. As I write this the memory of it all becomes clear as it blends into all the others. I must go now to contemplate my next endeavor. Cherish the wind or whatever you hold dear. Give my wife Cheryle my love. She will know it is I when she reads this. She knows how much I loved the wind.

Jerry 99

The Energy Of The Soul

I always thought my body was warm because I was a living human being. The blood coursing through my veins kept an inner heat going. There are many explanations for body heat. Now I hold one as true and it is not biological. It is the energy of the soul. The soul alone that keeps the body alive.

I can recall with great clarity every moment of death I have experienced. With each additional one it became less traumatic. There was a point where I recognized the start and would be able to take the ride heedlessly.

The first experience left me confused. I did not comprehend that the soul can leave the body anytime. However once you take it out it is very difficult to put it back. Thus I went too far a couple of times causing a demise of the current life.

Now that I have perfected the method I enjoy it more than birth.

We come to this place with apprehension. A sense of foreboding dominates the background. Learning to adapt the agility of spiritual form leaves us as we stumble about in a clay body of earth. Awkwardly making the steps towards evolution. Pray tell me who devised this dubious plan? By becoming dense we evolve? Why this physical form? Must we keep in the loop of repetition until we achieve perfection? These questions were the first from my lips after my death. Becoming bored, I turn to the light in hopes it will guide me. There is a leader to follow. Running I try to catch up for a glimpse of his face. Upon clear inspection I see for the first time the leader is me.

In this clarity I now see the delicate precise nature of the cycle. Truly an elaborate being proposed this plan.

I search for the author, again it is me.

After participation in many cycles perhaps the whole picture will become clear.

I leave you to your thoughts.

Me.

Stella

Dear Friend

I woke up alone. My heart felt fluttery in my chest. When I looked down I found that I had no body. So how could I feel a flutter. Panic swelled in what was left of me which I found was next to nothing. Incredible how I still felt whole. I no longer existed yet I was very alert. I could see everything, feel everything. All of my senses were intact. How can this be. I could see my body curled up in the corner. Discolored from the cold and death. Amazing that I looked rather peaceful, as if I had just taken a moment to rest. The winter had taken its toll. All of my family starved and froze to death in the new land.

A colony of England so arrogant in its inception, now gasping for life in the coldest winter any one ever knew. How ignorant we were. Not enough food and lodging so menial that it's a wonder we lasted as long as we did. Now I have no expectation to be physical. I must be dead. I appear to be so. I dart about looking for an answer. Could I be haunting this place? No one else is here. Where did their consciousness go? I can see their bodies also. All look the same as mine. Dead. I feel warmth. It should be cold. I wait.

No one comes. There are no survivors. I am alone. I amuse myself with thoughts of my childhood. Pleasant memories light a path around me and I feel love.

There is nothing else. All that is left to me is my memories. I have lost track of the days. Somehow day and night have blended together to become an endless existence. I've no where to go. It must be a very long time. Nothing changes. I wonder what will become of me. I pray to God but he does not answer. What to do. What to do.

I feel powerful but weak. I feel anger at my predicament. Surely there is an answer to this puzzle. Physical slips away and I wonder where my spiritual journey will take me. I've become bored with the inside of this cabin and its message of death. I step outside into the snow + starlight. The vastness of the air fills me and I feel exhilarated. I begin to rise so that I can pluck a star into my being. They are so beautiful. Higher + higher I climb.

I am engulfed in starlight. Each pinpoint of light becoming closer to me. As they get closer I see the life upon them. Eons of existence upon a pinpoint of starlight. All I have to do is pick one. I blend my essence to a unique one a little out of my path. It swirls towards me until I can make out what type of life exists upon it. I close my eyes and inhale its energy. I become one with the life force of this star. My energy embodied in a new life form. Different but after so long of boredom a welcome thing indeed. I am reborn. Reborn to a new life. Another chance for evolution. I am pleased. I live.

Stella

Dear Friend
I woke up alone. My heart felt fluttery in my chest. When I looked down I found that I had no body so how could I

...

Stella

Tia

Dear friend,

The winter wind whistles around the outside corner of my room. Icicles cling to the edge of my window sill in hopes of touching the ground with their tips. I sit in the window wrapped in my warmest robe. The display of cold an everlasting video of entertainment. As the wind turns brisker I see the people rushing to and fro from their days. I recall living life like that. I still do inside my head. My body however has slowed somewhat. I no longer rush anywhere. The withered limbs I used to call legs are now wrapped neatly under a blanket. I spend most of my time sitting in this wheel chair watching the world go by. I think I had a birthday a while back. Somewhere around ninety I believe. In my soul I am still young and vital. I go to the tunnel everyday to visit. Greeted by angelic friends who know who I really am. We spend the sunny days with a picnic. Fried chicken all my favorites. I only come back to the icicles and my chair when I have to. Like when someone insists on an answer to a question. Then I snap to. My friends asked me to stay longer today. There was going to be a bonfire on the beach and they wanted me to join them. Could I? I did not really know who would really care if I did not go back. I was having so much fun. I couldn't resist.

To be back in my body calculating time was awful. I made note to not do that again. It was time to be placed in bed for the evening. A double attendant job to be sure. Once I was ready I looked over at the window and saw beads of precipitation on the window. Perhaps it was warming up. I decided to return to the bonfire. So what if returning was difficult. The party lasted way into the wee hours. I made the attempt to slip into bed but was unable to. Panic began to set in. My body inert was clammy + cold to the touch. What was going on here?

I sat holding my hand until the sun came thru the blinds. Starring at my face I realized that I really did not know who this was. It was merely a costume of sorts. One I had worn for very long. Now it was tired and I was not. I still wanted to go to bonfires and play on the beach in the sun. Reluctantly I let go of my hand. I would miss the person I was this time. I would miss the icicles and the frosty scene of life before me. However a fresh start awaited me in the sunlight. I turned to the tunnel. I was ready to go. I never looked back on my way to the beach. No regrets. I would spend some time contemplating what I would do next. Perhaps a warmer climate. Perhaps a different path. I don't know. Guess I'll sit here in the sand until I figure it out.

Tia

AmbrosE

Dear friend,

I grasp the arm of the chair in an effort to retrieve the strength so quickly draining out of my body. Foolishly hoping within the grasp that somehow my life energy will hold here a bit longer. It's funny how when it's time to cross a line I suddenly become very fearful. Now in these few moments fleeting through me I realize how foolish the fear was. Or should I say "is". I suppose the moment has arrived to where I should say the line has been crossed. It's a wonder to me that I feel no difference. All that fear was for naught. Instead of hearing I am sensing in its deepest form. I feel like laughing at the absurdity of the situation. Here I am having crossed the most major line of this existence and it was more like a burp from root beer than a catastrophe. I _am_ still somewhere. Of course that's not why I write to you. I write because it's important for you to understand that it is essential for one to cross the line while existing on the earth plane.

So many events in this past life of mine would have been altered if I had crossed the line with boldness & assurance. Instead my choice was submission.

162

Now having retrieved the sum of that life's equation I find boldness would have made a difference.

Be mindful that there were many lessons learned on this path I followed, but crossing the line would have enhanced my evolution considerably.

We all have many paths leading to the direction of our destiny. I guess by writing this I am crossing the line to you in hopes that my experience will somehow alter your path. Alter it enough for you to cross the line into a bold new awareness. Death is not what you suppose. It's not an ascension to the light, it's not an ending to a drama. There are many things it is not and I could go to eternity with them. I'll tell you what it is though. It is a major line crossing that should not be feared. The fear can be eliminated by beginning to cross minor lines placed by you & others in your earth plane existence on a daily basis.

I am pleased with the opportunity to dictate this letter. It is the one true line I have crossed and the boldness of the endeavor leaves me giddy with accomplishment.

As you read it please open your mind to the possibility that indeed it is possible. Imagine what a great line crossing it would be.

Yours sincerely

AmbrosE

Bobcat

Dear friend

It hurts! It hurts so much that I cannot utter a sound. My mouth is open but nothing but air escapes. There is a turbulence in my mind whirling about making futile attempts at comfort. Perhaps if my body stops breathing the cessation of movement will freeze the moment and there will be no pain. Is it working? Will it stop?...No it will not. With a final intake of breath I gaze down at this body through clouded eyes. The visual leaves me more paralyzed than I could have ever imagined. This must be what shock is. Rigidly I move my hand to the arrow protruding from my chest. Of course it's so obvious. Remove it! Take it back to where it came from. Retrieve the moment and make it different so that the pain will cease to exist. Alas it cannot be so. Moments cannot be retrieved. Once an arrow is shot it will make its path to its destination. In doing so wreaking havoc upon its target.

My hand laces its fingers around the shaft. With trembling ambition I attempt the removal. Focusing on the wounded area I begin to realize that indeed it is quite all right. No need to hurry. The last bit of breath

165

that passes from my lips leaves as a smile is formed. It does not hurt now. In the calm I am able to experience this situation more clearly. An arrow has pierced my heart. The final beat occurring only moments ago. The release of panic allows me now to see the purpose in this exchange. The arrow is an accumulation of all the remarks I made with a dagger consistency throughout this life. By continuing this type of behavior I manifested all of them into a physical arrow that now has pierced my heart & soul. It's funny but I feel no remorse only the knowledge & understanding necessary to move forward and repair what I have done.

I look now at this body so important a moment ago and realize with a laugh that it deserved what it created. All of my arrows shot throughout an ambitious life caused more pain than what I experienced. My message to you if you care to listen is this: You will always feel the tip of an arrow shot for what ever reason. In my case it manifested itself into the physical and ultimately ended one of my lives. Now I must repeat the lesson.

Sincerely

Bobcat

1857

Stewart

Dear Friend,

I remember the flash of light then the silence. In that silence there has been plenty of time for reflection and the filing of events that have led to this. What is this, you ask? The question has burned inside me since my arrival. The silence is what has grabbed me close and forcibly made me reconstruct my path. Visions & memories of events, friends, & family have visited me to keep me company. Those visits have kept me sane. The silly dramas, the passing of dates, have kept me entertained & comforted in the silence.

How long have I been here? I don't remember and somehow it seems irrelevant. The only consistency is the silence. I am unable to create anything other than the remembrance of already created events. This is baffling to me. I know instinctively that I was able to do so before. There was a life I was living I know it. The constructed walls of my reality so sturdy are now flimsy at best. It occurred to me that I must be dead. So does that make this hell? Or is it heaven? I think not.

If I am deceased there should be something here. I have consciousness. Shouldn't there be someone to meet me? Nothing but silence. Time for reflection on what? Scrolling through the scenes of my life there is indeed a pattern. I was very adept at creating whatever I wanted. My reality was filled with activity and a buzz of energy. I don't remember how it was done but I did it. There is nothing to do here but the continuous movie of my life over and over. I don't get it.

Silence & more silence lulls me into a relaxed state until I seemingly find myself again in the drama of my life. Have I escaped? No. I realize after more silence that I never appreciated my ability to create newness in my existence. My lack of appreciation has led me to the place of silence. By meditating on the subject I have allowed my self the realization that I should be more appreciative of my abilities on the earth plane. I found it hard to believe but I was creating the silence so I would actually hear myself think. Damn. I am good.

Hopefully you my friend will find some values in my experience. Appreciate your creative abilities and honor them. I plan to…no, I will next time.

Stewart

Dear friend

I remember the flash of light then the silence.

...

value in my experience Appreciate your creative abilities and honor them. I plan to l... no I will next time

Stewart

Coloring Between The Lines

My Dear Friend,

As I walk through the lush garden of my essence creation, I can feel drops of moisture on my cheeks. The soft patter of their droplets pound out a rhythm that resembles passages in my life. As they increase in speed they become a melody of what was and now shall ever be, this life pattern that sifts softly through my lessons. The grass beneath my feet glides like a velvet blanket. In this clear moment of evaluation I realize the one error of this drama. Something so simple but so intricate in my process towards understanding. I realize now that this one thought was projected to me many more times than I could ever count. It was a quiet comment from an even more quiet woman, whispered in a fleeting moment of intimacy. Now as I stand on the threshold of a new beginning, I turn back to share this one comment of importance. Back towards the voice begging me to stay. Back to the moment before. Back to those so involved in my drama. How do I tell them what should be said? Will they understand? Will they put it to use? Did I?

As I approach the end of the tunnel the last steps become most impossible. Grasping the hand in mine I open my eyes. They are all still there, living the drama I have chosen to leave. If I had listened to the quiet comment perhaps I should be at the end of another great stage play. However, all that is left is the opportunity to be the quiet woman with an ever so quiet comment. It is my last effort. You see when I was small and fresh in the mind of my parents the quiet woman sought to free me of the bonds of this particular drama. I was careful and what was presented was what I applied. I was taught to color within the lines. A simple task but expected nevertheless. The quiet woman sought to encourage me to ignore the lines. To be bold and color when I wished not what was predetermined for me.

It is the single most important lesson that one could ever learn.

So it is my desire with my last breath of sweet life to tell you. Do not color within the lines.

I feel heaviness in my chest, it's time to go. Hopefully you will understand the message. Turning I move towards the entrance of the tunnel. The quiet woman stands at the entrance smiling. It appears that I did fulfill this life. I was to tell you about coloring between those lines. Smiling from deep inside, I again

walk the lush garden of my essence. Only this time I
am not alone. And I dream of you coloring at random
the evolution of your essence.

Life is Now

Dear friend:

Just a quick note for I really am busy today. Run here, run there. I'm sure you understand. I simply don't have enough time anymore. It seems there's always some issue pressing, pushing me into the next moment before I can take a breath.

Remember the filled agenda I spoke to you about? Well multiply it by two dear. I'm making plans to slow down after the first of the year. Really I am. The kids go back to school on the 7th and Bill & I are going to spend some time together. That is if I finish all the projects planned at work. Well dear just wanted to touch base.

Talk to you soon

Me

Dear friend

Sorry I haven't written, work has been lethal. The proposal I pitched to the advertisement company was accepted. You know what that means...no rest for the wicked! It looks like the Holidays will take a backseat this year. It doesn't look like I'll be able to come see you after all. Perhaps after the 7th after Bill & I make our time. Oh that's right, it won't be the right time then either. Busy, Busy, Busy. Promise to write soon.

Me

Dear friend,

Before you scold me for not writing, let me tell you. After the 7th Bill had to run to the coast for a very important meeting so our plans fell through, which was actually fine because work became so hectic I was losing my mind anyway. The kids are fine but we're all too busy to meet with you next month. If my schedule clears I'll let you know.

Me.

Dear friend.

Sorry I missed your party. Bill & I are trying to juggle more business agendas and the kids are involved in a series of events at school. Look I promise we'll see you at Easter. Things should be slowed down a bit by then.

Me

Dear friend.

I'm sorry. No wait...I've made so many apologies over my lifetime. There was never enough time. I don't know what happened. Thank you for the flowers you sent. I really did not deserve them. In my haste to slide through life I missed the point. Life is more than a series of future events to be lived through. Life is now. This breath. This moment. I regret not spending one present moment with you.

In my projections onto events, I deluded myself into believing that indeed the future was fulfilling my desire to spend time with you.

Now I see the truth. As I gaze down watching you weep at my funeral, I wonder how you can. What did I share with you? A hope!? A promise of a future moment spent. Hopefully somewhere you will read this and learn from it. Live in this moment not promises of the next.

Cling to the truth of your life in this moment. It may be all you ever have. I await the next opportunity to experience life with you, and take comfort in knowing it will be different.

Me

Unlock Your Soul

Dear Friend

I remember your tears as the vision of you faded from my sight. My first reaction was one of panic and concern. Panic in not knowing where I was going and concern for your eyes and the pain they held. I never wanted to see you so hurt. I could feel your fingertips as they passed over my face. The salty taste of your tears on my lips as they ceased moving. It was such an odd sensation this dying, not at all what I expected.

When I was young there were tales of a grim reaper with that horror film genre our world created. I guess that's what I was expecting. What a surprise to meet no one. Well no one I knew at least. There were essences surrounding me but I was locked for a time in your embrace of grief.

Because it was familiar I took comfort in it and built a reality around it. Since there is no measure of time I was there for a brief moment and eternity. Your tears awakened a form of my self that relived the final moment searching for a way to rewrite the ending of my life.

When someone finally approached me I was submerged in the thought of your grief. Attempting to cleanse your soul of despair I missed the point.

Yes there is a point in death. Fortunately I was able to unlock myself from that circle of reality. By doing so I also released you from this odd commitment.

Live my friend and experience all that physical life has to offer. Your tears remain on my lips but they now nourish my essence into a new existence. I await the moment when you enter this space. I remember your face and I wallow in the essence of your love. It all exists here...and there...Everywhere. We are all timeless and eternal.

Unlock your soul. I await you with an open heart.

Love

    Me

George

Dear Martha

I bring tidings of joy. It appears that I am suddenly able to chew properly. There were red succulent apples across the glen. I remember consoling myself that I would be at least able to sample some of its sauce. However, upon approaching I found myself biting immediately hence into the apple. Now thou remember that it has been many years since I was able to do thus. Imagine if you will my amazement at the initial bite. A spray of juice encompassed my tongue none the fresher than in that initial bite. It was a memory long ago tucked away suddenly unfolding in my present. An apple bite, the miracle of my old age. After chewing it suddenly occurred to me that I was actually biting and chewing. How long has it been since I was able to do that! Was I dreaming or did I miss something along the way? Why was there no pain? Why was it apparently all right? What was not revealed? Completely engrossed in the apple I conveniently left caution and reason to the wind and completed my taking of the apple.

It became apparent that there was something awry with this scenario. It was clouding my immense enjoyment of the apple biting. It was something sorely missed in recent years. The initial bite of a ripe apple a remnant of my youth and a firm body.

Now a miracle. More apples abundantly appearing. I was able to eat them with a hearty bite. No slicing. No neatly delicately taking with the front teeth that could somehow not relish the essence of the apple. With youthful abandonment I consumed many more.

My love it was intoxicating looking down immersed in my apple. A joy denied for so long. But perchance why in this moment is it available? Perchance I have died and went to heaven. Perchance not.

However, the delicate aroma of apples has distracted me thus again. I will await you while eating. You will come soon or late. Your choice. In the meantime I will await you. With apple of course grinding on all of my solid teeth. You know they are real. I just bit into another.

Adieu

George

Joshua

Dear friend

The coverlets you have pulled close to my feeble body bring me great comfort. I recognize the top layer. It was a gift for my wedding so many years ago. Amazing how durable it has been for these many years. There is not a thread undone. How I wish I could be in still such good condition. My hand traces the pattern of lace embroidered into the edge. It feels like a warm friend here to comfort me on my journey to the heavens. Oh it's allright. I know I am dying. I know the moments grow fewer with each breath into these old lungs. How kind of you to sit with me during the transition.

As I inhale the stale air of this sickroom it puzzles me that you should pick these final moments to sit with me. I am pleased at your dedications. Your hand feels cool upon my forehead. Somehow it relieves the dull ache in my bones. How unfair that dying should be so painful. It should be a joyous time. A coming home of sorts. I am not pleased that I endure such discomfort. However your presence dulls the pain somewhat. If I could still speak I would thank you for your presence, since I cannot I write this letter to you in hopes that somehow you will receive it.

The night air is chilly and the coverlet warms my cooling body but soon it will lose its battle. I feel the energy of my soul slowly stepping away from this form. If I were alone I would be a little fearful. Moving forward into something so different I find myself motionless. Then I feel your hands as they smooth the coverlets & your voice whispering your love. I feel energized with new strength and adventure. Thank you for staying. Though it appears I travel alone, your love is my mantle of courage. I leave this body without fear thanks to you.

This is why I write to you from another place of being. To let you know how important your energy was to my stepping into the cosmos unafraid.

Thank you.

Your vigil was the single most loving gift I ever received.

Joshua.

Simplicity

Dear Friend

Come to my memorial a week from tomorrow. I'll be counting the moments 'till you do. A bad habit I picked up while in physical form. You probably do not recognize my writing for now it has more texture and form. Kind of like me. Oh! It's such a tremendous adventure this place. A manifestation of all my fantasies and dreams. I never realized how detailed they were.

Remember how we used to talk about death and all of the options? Well you won't believe it. <u>All</u> of the options were valid. Pretty wild. Come to my memorial. I will try to give you some physical sign. I have been advised that you most likely will not be able to focus clearly enough to notice. However I wish to try.

I should attempt to give you some insight as to where I am but it's so simple I do not know where to begin. No that's not true. I do know where but it's too simple for you to acknowledge.

That is the mystery—the simplicity. We all tried to complicate the intricacies. Look. By writing this in human cursive I've already complicated it. I know you will not completely understand.

Come to the memorial. I will attempt simplicity.

See you then

Me

Adrienne

I have held pain so long in my bosom that the absence of it leaves me alone and empty. I first noticed the void when I got up last evening to go to the bathroom. Normally that could be quite an ordeal. My feet hit the floor and I braced my self for the initial burst of discomfort. Surprised at the absence I made my way to the bathroom. Although the lights were out I was able to see quite clearly. My eyes are still in good shape. It's the rest of me that is in shambles.

The linoleum felt cool on my feet. A pleasant sensation that surprised me by remaining pleasant. Normally the pain blinds me to the simple things. Crawling back in the sheets I experienced no difficulties. I remember chuckling to myself that there was still some fight left in the old girl. Pulling the covers up to my chin I waited for the pain to return. It didn't. Its absence kept my eyes awake until the sun came up. I felt like I had been robbed of a part of myself, realizing now how much pain had dominated my existence. And now it was gone.

Feeling a bit pissed I attempted to sit up. In doing so I felt a slight jolt and release. This hospital bed could use some repair. I rang for the nurse repeatedly.

Where were they? Didn't they realize I was a sick woman and needed help?!

I swung my legs over the side of the bed. No pain? I shuffled to the door - still no pain. I opened the door and looked down the hall. No pain? Perhaps we had been invaded and I was the last person on the planet. How ridiculous. Everyone was going about their business. No one noticed me. How strange? I hadn't been out of that bed for a very long time. Surely my appearance would be an oddity.

I made a mental note to put in a complaint about the aloofness of the hospital staff. Everyone just looked through me. Here I am a very sick woman out of bed for the first time in months and no one seemed to care.

I plodded back to my room very pissed indeed, the door swinging easily and I was stunned at the picture before me. There I was still in bed eyes closed asleep. I could hear a clock ticking from off in the distance. Counting off time which of course now was irrelevant to me.

Suddenly I got it. A new sense of reality descended upon me and I was transformed. I am now on a new journey to a new place. I just wanted to let some one know. There's so much more.

Adrienne

In This Moment

Dear friend

The light of the fire should be growing dim. Hours have passed since I lit the first kindling. It seems that the moment has expanded becoming more than just a blink in time. A fascinating experience I might add. So many moments such as this one I would pay a king's ransom for. The technique would be a quite marketable commodity. Ah...but let us get back to the fire. The hearth still radiates a fresh warmth. You know the kind where the frosty feeling gradually blends away. The precise moment is what is perpetuating here. I suppose there should be a feeling of something amiss. However the fear connected to such a thing cannot materialize fully.

Upon inspection I find the walls the same and unchanged. All of my belongings are in order. The plush feel of the carpet still caresses my feet. My gaze locked upon the flames fantasizes about a life just ending and yet beginning. Confused I walk over to the door. Perhaps some crisp night air will help me focus. Focus? Focus on what? The moment is all there is. To lock onto anything else would be useless. Why do I feel this way?

My mind is blurred by images of the past. They all roll together as they tumble through the fire. On and on they roll right through the present into a future. Unable to put all the facts together I decide to gaze into the fire. In this moment I realize that the moment is eternal and I have come home. This space is a creation that lives for me in the now.

Yes my friend the reality we shared is now from a different perspective. I guess you could say I have died. The fire is a symbol of the life force inside. This is my truth and I felt compelled to share with you.

I don't remember how I got here...only the fire sustains me.

I will await your arrival in this place by the fire. When you catch up it will be warmer and more inviting. A dual creation always is. Look for me. I will watch for you.

<u>Me</u>

Dear friend

The light of the fire should be growing dim. Hours have passed since I lit the first kindling. It seems that the moment has expanded becoming more than just a blink in time. A fascinating experience I might add.

...

I will await your arrival in this place by the fire. When you catch up it will be warmer and more inviting. A dual creation always is. Look for me. I will watch for you.

MC

Daphne

Dear Friend,

I am writing so that you will not worry. Each moment that torments you ripples to me like an ocean wave. That's the best way to describe it I suppose. A description of where I am is not the real purpose of this letter. However, the opportunity to share it with you is exciting. If I am able to keep writing I will do so.

Let me address your worry or should I say guilt. My passing from one place to another was a plan of my own. Nothing you did precipitated my choice. Remember that phrase: My choice. Existence is a plan that we create in all forms of life. I merely decided to change. I know that you blame yourself for my situation. Yes, you were involved in the drama as an actor but ultimately remember I was the director. The grand plan was that we would come away with some insight on our relationship. It was not meant to throw you into a whirlpool of guilt and shame.

Physical pain is but a dim memory to me now. Yes in those last moments it was difficult but the pain was meant to give us clarity. I know it sounds strange but in my position the clarity survives and is useful. Please know that the lesson learned was appreciation. Mutual appreciation. It certainly was not to be one of guilt. My hope is that this note will allow you to see that your guilt will only cloud your real purpose.

Your presence at my passing was an indicator that you finally got it! Do not allow anything to diminish that.

I rejoice at the opportunity to tell you. I am fine. Different but more than whole as we knew it. Live your life with this positive lesson. I will wait for you. The window is closing...

Daphne

Your Big Brother

DEAR FRIEND,

REMEMBER WHEN WE USED TO JUMP ON DAD'S BED? WE MUST HAVE BEEN ABOUT 2 OR 3 YEARS OLD. THERE WAS ALSO ANOTHER TIME WHEN WE WENT TO A FESTIVAL WHERE THERE WAS AN ACTUAL TRAMPOLINE. WE BEGGED FATHER FOR THE 10 CENTS TO JUMP ON IT. I CAN STILL SEE YOUR EYES WIDE OPEN AS WE WENT HIGHER + HIGHER. BIG BROWN EYES. MY POINT TO THIS STORY IS TO JOGGLE YOUR MEMORY. I WOULD VERY MUCH LIKE FOR YOU TO RECALL HOW YOU FELT AS YOU JUMPED HIGHER + HIGHER. ESPECIALLY ON THE WAY UP. FOR ME IT WAS A FEELING OF EXPANSION. I CAN IDENTIFY IT NOW. MY INSIDES FELT BIGGER. THE SCREAM OF GLEE CAME FROM DEEP INSIDE ME. REMEMBER HOW MUCH FUN IT WAS? WE HELD HANDS WHEN YOU BECAME A LITTLE SCARED. REMEMBER? YOU SAID MY HAND MADE YOU FEEL OKAY. WE ACTUALLY WENT MUCH HIGHER WHEN WE WENT TOGETHER.

CLOSE YOUR EYES AND REMEMBER. LOOK FOR MY HAND, IT'S STILL THERE. DO NOT BE AFRAID. WE STILL CAN GO HIGHER TOGETHER. I WILL ALWAYS BE READY TO TAKE YOUR HAND. DEATH IS LIKE JUMPING ON THE TRAMPOLINE. I KNOW. I HAVE ALREADY MADE THE LEAP. I WILL NOT ABANDON YOU NOW. TAKE MY HAND WHEN YOU ARE READY AND WE WILL JUMP TOGETHER.

YOUR BIG BROTHER,

ME.

Focus

Dear friend

Hopeless.

Hopeless and alone.

That is the feeling inside when I was waiting for the end to come. Each moment compounded into many more. Endlessly multiplying until I couldn't even see them anymore. Truly despondent I wallowed in my misery. Lapping up my bad misfortune like a cup of milk before bed. Being told that misery loves company became my national anthem. What a life. What a misery. What a waste.

I can say that now. Having gone through the whole scene I can make statements concerning my lack of progress in that particular life. Perhaps I should feel ashamed, but I don't. The lessons learned during my marriage to misery are invaluable.

When I first realized my death I was out in the garden. Of course nothing I ever planted grew properly. There was always something amiss. Looking to the heavens I cursed the universe for my misery. The pestilence of bad misfortune hung like a ball & chain around my neck. On this particular morning however I noticed that the tomatoes were rather red & luscious. Surprised I stood motionless waiting for a bird or what not to destroy it. When nothing happened I reached down to pick one. It was immediately replaced by another. I knew something was up.

There was a drop of moisture on one of the leaves that looked peculiar. Upon closer inspection I found I could see a reflection of myself in the leaf. Curious. The image was a young version of me. The me in the leaf began to talk to the me in the garden. Now I was sure I was dead or something.

The image told a story about me that made sense. Creation is a tricky process. In each life we create that which is perfect for our growth. It may not always make sense but you have to look at the big picture. In my case I became entranced with one small misery. I gave it all my focus and of course it multiplied. Pretty simple ending for a complicated life. Imagine if I had focused on something else. Now I know I can create what ever I want. I am not at the mercy of anything but myself. Oddly enough only a version of me could have told me this.

Misery is something I will not duplicate again. When it comes my way I will focus on something else. Perhaps another garden, a fruitful one this time.

197

'Hope you read this in the middle of misery. Perhaps it will help.

Me

Giving

Dear friend,

The smell of perspiration clings to my nostrils as I slide slowly to the floor. It is really humorous to me that my last thoughts would be wondering why these guys do not bathe properly. There should be pain somewhere but my body is numb. I cannot feel anything. The floor boards feel splintery on my arms. It's a shame I never got around to sanding them. As my head hits the floor I feel a tidal wave of nausea that goes nowhere. I suppose in my numbness there is no place for it to go.

Fear should have enveloped me when they caught me, however defeat can be a powerful drug. Giving up seemed like the only alternative. Closing my eyes I can remember the sound only. I deserved to die. I was a thief and they were the robbers. Pretty much the same thing if you think about it. We were all the bad guys. It never occurred to me that I would end my life as I live it. Violently.

Now that I can see it with more clarity, I realize that life and your actions in it are a careful balance. In my haste to have it all I missed some important issues.

My whole life was a series of ups & downs. Mostly downs. I was poor and thought those with the money had the power. I saw those taking taking taking and never giving back. I grew up doing just that. Never balancing the take with give. Of course now I get it after I find my self bleeding & dead on the floor of my mama's shed.

Too bad I could not have learned the lesson in the physical. I can remember the trigger man's eyes. They wanted to take. Now I wish I could have given him this knowledge.

That is why I write, so that you will give it to someone who needs it. By your giving perhaps you will begin a new process. I know that this letter has changed my process. Next time it will be different. I get it.

<u>Me</u>

Dear friend,

The smell of perspiration clings to my nostrils as I slide slowly to the floor. It is really humorous to me that my last thoughts would be wondering why these guys do not breathe properly. There should

. . .

That is why I write. So that you will give it to someone who needs it. By your giving perhaps you will begin a new process. I know that this letter has changed my process. Next time it will be different. I get it.

Me

Opportunity Exists In The Now

Dear Friend,

When the end came it was so abrupt that it knocked me off my feet. There was no pain. No warning, no time. There were moments of reenactment. Stuff I remember happening but had forgotten all the minute details. Now they came forward like a fresh line of ideas. Manifesting themselves one upon another. I was a participant on so many levels I'm not sure I could ever explain it to you. I found comfort in the moments thinking that it was all a dream. Surely when the sun came up it would all be a faded memory.

They tell me that I was in that state for eternity and a moment. I guess it's all about one's point of view. And that viewpoint is why I am writing to you now.

There were many plans made for the life I lived while knowing you. I was great at the future but lousy in the present. By betting on what I would do in the future I thought I was buying time. There was the error. The future I was planning for, the me I was going to be never existed. They were cut off when the blood clot hit my brain. Gone. Dead. Done.

You see by viewing my life from the future I enabled my self to be satisfied with where & what I was. Not that there was anything drastically wrong with me. You know I was a pretty good guy. I just had a wrong angle on my view.

One exists in the now. Any growth becomes available only by accessing what exists right now. The future can never really be until you get there. To pretend your future self is you now would rob you of spiritual growth. Please use my error as a stepping stone for your present self.

Physical life is but a glimmer in what I know now. It is precious and it is immediate. Do not delay anything of importance until tomorrow. That is the lesson. Of course there are many lessons to learn & physical existences to live. We thought only to tell you since this writing opportunity presented its self to us in our now. We thank the channel. And we thank you my friend for reading.

Go in peace.

Me.

Do Not Let Fear Chase You

My little one.

This opportunity presents itself oddly in my now existence. I was not expecting a chance for a physical voice ever and certainly not in this way. The others who greeted me understood my grief and told me of many ways to separate myself from negativity. Again, that is a complicated story and best left for the time being. This moment is for communicating my love for you and to attempt explanation for my actions. Please keep reading for my voice is silent. Only your eyes can hear my confessions. Perhaps confession is a bit dramatic but the telling will cleanse my heart of regret. This cleansing perhaps will give us both an opportunity to accept what happened and to live on in forgiveness.

The time we spent in the physical was beautiful. Your eyes caught me the moment you were born. They felt like they bore completely into my soul. Those eyes were those of an old soul. There are legends of old souls in our culture. It is said they have lived many lives and bring to the present life wisdom beyond that of normal souls, such as myself.

You were special. Oh so special and I was your birth mother. Your mom. I had never held something so precious in my arms before. It was over powering. My goal was to be everything for you. I recognized my gift and was prepared to raise you to be the wise sage you were predestined to be.

Time progressed and there were many "firsts". Your first tooth, first step, first word. So many that now it seems every moment was a first.

You blossomed. It was deeply satisfying to watch you grow. The smell of your hair left me breathless. Your laugh made me feel like the whole world was at my command. I can now only remember the moment it all began to go wrong. My self doubt creeping in like a thief to steal our sunny days. Questions coming to the surface of my consciousness that clouded my judgment and made me feel unworthy. You see you were so special and I was not. Writing it now gives me clarity. In that time I was misguided and fearful. I began to drink alcohol to "find God." How self serving in retrospect. However, we are all accountable for our actions and I take responsibility for those poor choices.

The night it happened you were sleeping so peacefully. I cried in the moonlight admiring your innocence. My guilt over my unworthiness growing larger and larger until the bedroom suddenly disappeared from view. Who knows where I got the pistol. Protection was the excuse I used. Little did I know the greatest enemy lurked within my own delusional fear. Looking back I do not remember pulling the trigger. It just happened in nickelodeon fashion, one scene after another. I heard your little piggy bank crack from the bullet. I couldn't even eliminate my self with any accuracy.

As my vision clouded I saw those beautiful eyes of yours begin to tremble from within. My last thought was the realization that you would blame yourself. But then of course it was too late.

So now I write to you from another place. I have tamed the fears that distorted my path in the life I shared with you. My friends here have helped me regain my worth. I am whole. And this opportunity to write to you has been a blessing. Please take my love with you from this life to the next. Do not blame yourself for my fears. They had nothing to do with you. Look fear in the eye with boldness. Do not let it chase you into a dark corner. Instead remember my love.

We will have more sunny days.

Me (Mom)

TESSiE

Dear friend

What a peculiar sensation. I grip the pen in unison with this person. A person of whom I never met in life, or at least not one of recent memory. It is said here that in my acceptance I will receive more realizations of my whole self. For now though the experience is odd none the less. It crosses my mind how in my naiveté I never knew of these things I experience now. Religion was very much a formula to be followed. Filled with ritual and images said to be too sacred to behold. It strikes me now that religion was just a way to pacify the real longing for what is here. I know you are waiting for a description of just what "here" is. If there were words to sing its praises I would write a melody. I very much would tell you the lyrics so that you could create your own song, your own heaven. Heaven is what you are hoping I say. A place where all is forgiven and there is reunion with those you've loved. A day of sunshine so brilliant accompanied by a perfect warm evening surrounded by twinkling stars and a full moon. These things I would give you if I could. However in my continual evolution in this place it suddenly occurs to me that you must create your own place, your own salvation, your own heaven. I cannot give them to you.

Once you leave physical form the rules are not changed, only enhanced. If you perceived one minute moment of your own power in the physical heaven will be at your finger tips "here".

The touch of physical fingers mingled with my own, grip this pen in hopes you hear me. I am still "here" just not "there". There is so much to tell and such a small window of opportunity. There is a vast space waiting for each person. Waiting to be molded into something of your choosing. The best way to prepare is to practice creating what you want there. My desire to communicate with you manifested this physical hand to write this letter. I am "here". My future is one with my "now" with you. We realize an understanding is still in front of you. Take comfort in the knowledge I am creating and expanding my universe in hopes that when you are finally "here" I will be the one to guide you. The window closes now but be assured we await another opportunity.

Remember this.

Me.

TESSiE

Balance

Dear friend

I saw you today or at least I thought I did. There have been many visions passing before my overly active eyes, but the sight of you prompted a response. I actually remember only meeting you once while alive. It was a brief encounter but one of great significance for both of us. The interaction inspired by my arrogance left you feeling less about yourself as a being. Truly it was not my intention but a result of a pattern well engraved in who I was then. Now that I have viewed all the arrogant dramas played out in my life I can appreciate the impact it had upon you & others who crossed my path.

When I first arrived here my vision was clouded and my being still enclosed in my arrogance. Upon meditation the ramifications of what I had done to others overwhelmed me beyond despair. Only in that deep pit of astonishment & disbelief was I able to realize that atonement was necessary. You might have a different religious background of that I am not sure but please realize that no matter what end is met, there is always the need of ultimate balance.

The others have been helpful in my process, something I would have never done for them. Well I guess that would be different now. By seeing you today I rejoice in the knowledge that I am beginning to create a process by which I can balance out all my previous life actions. The warmth of your essence touches mine and I can feel your forgiveness. This is a true blessed event. Thank you and thank yourself for a balance co-created.

I saw you today and it was good. Your essence glows brightly as mine now is becoming.

Thank you.

Me

Better Choices

Dear friend

Distant in my memory there is a feeling of warmth and solidity. There were moments in my previous life where I approached that moment but through poor choices it alluded me. Now that I have stopped measuring time I find that there is suddenly a vast amount of it that can never be measured. Part of me would like to look at that more closely but I realize the senselessness of that endeavor. There is no time. I know my focus should stay with solidity. That was my problem in the physical. A lack of focus perpetuated the many not so great choices I made. They tell me here that there are not any poor choices for each one no matter what, leads you down a path of learning. I still find fault with that concept. Spending many moments berating my self for mistakes that caused a delay in my progress.

Through the physical manifestation of this letter I have achieved the ultimate focus. To blend through a physical form not my own requires great concentration. I have attempted this process many times without success. They have told me here that this achievement allows for many "good" events to unfold. I am honored to participate and I offer thanks for the opportunity to "focus".

As the writing continues the feeling of warmth & solidity moves closer. Thank you. I feel perhaps that an era of better choices awaits me.

Thanks again.

Me

I've Something To Tell You

Dear friend,

I've something to tell you. As I gather the thoughts around me there is an urgency to put them in some kind of order so that it will be sensible. The order is critical as the thoughts in a pattern will create exactly what you need to know. Again I've something to tell you. Come close & listen.

When I walked the earth dimension so long ago my ego only allowed me to give credit to those things that were tangible. By that I mean my belief system only included that which I could touch in the physical. Life was in the moment and when it was gone so was I. There is no memory of how I came upon that conclusion. It just was and that was the end of it. Consequently as I aged a fear began to grow like a seedling inside my soul. I had nourished only my physical side as I believed that there was nothing after my physical death. So why bother. Upon the age of eight score and four I realized that the life I had so desperately clung to was about to end. The fear of imminent annihilation paralyzed my final moments.

The grasp so tightly upon my throat I was unable to speak to anyone about it.

The idea that my existence was so insignificant that it would just end began to plague every thing around me. What would it feel like in the final moment? All of my thoughts and feelings snuffed out of the physical in a brief moment. The world continuing on with out me. Perhaps a brief moment of remembrance and then continuing on in its same rambling fashion. The only thing left of me would be some decaying bones and a cold stone marker. Chilling.

There was no one to talk to in those final days. I lay on my bed ready to greet death with courage. The courage however left me on that last day. Sobbing into my pillow I allowed fear to grip me so heavily that I lost all sense of myself. The moment went on for a brief eternity. There was nothing. Just darkness and a hollow sense of aloneness that I never expected. So sad to be dead and over.

Dead and over lasted, that is until I lifted my head from my fear and despair. That one lifting was so easy I became embarrassed at my lack of energy. I looked around at familiar faces all smiling that I had allowed myself to arrive.

I guess I had been there all along and they were all waiting for me to allow my thoughts to create again. You see death is as easy as you want to be. The same principle of thought creating reality exists here also. In fact it is much more powerful. As I sheepishly stood among those who loved me the realization of creation of my after life hit home. So you see how important it is that which I have to tell you.

Do not allow fear of nothingness to hold you. For if you do that is exactly what you will have after death...nothing.

You can begin anytime to formulate that which you would like to have. It's all there in you. And you can create anything you want.

Yes that is what I had to tell you. I must return now to my after life. There is much to do.

Me

I Hope Someone Reads This Before They Die

Dear friend

I hear voices very near. It puzzles me that they are quite loud yet I am unable to decipher what is being said. My surroundings are very basic and bland. It looks rather like a prison cell yet there are not any bars. I write this note in hopes some one will find it. The length of my stay escapes me. There is no distinct memory of before my incarceration. I surely do not know what the future holds. There is only now and I am an unwilling player in this game.

I wonder in the night if my scratchings on the wall will survive. You see I write my letter on a wall of stone. I read somewhere (I am not sure when or where) that ancient writings have been found and that the messages left by a long gone culture survived for thousands of years. It is my hope my letter will survive.

In the empty space when I think too much many images fill my mind. Who are my captors? Why am I here? Why am I not hungry?

The bed on which I rest is covered with cotton bedding of white. The walls are white. The floor is white even the molding on the door is white. I have studied every crevasse of this room and have come up with nary a clue.

I am unable to remember exactly who I am. The voices slip centimeters from my ears frustrating me so. There is a hope that I will hear what they are saying. Perhaps they will lift this veil of ignorance.

Sh Sh h h h…they are approaching…It has occurred to me that I am insane. The voices speak of awareness, and forgiveness. Surely I am insane. This place must be an asylum. The voices become more audible and I surmise that one is male and one female. The female speaks brokenly of family and my inability to accept something. Yes I am indeed insane. The male provokes my senses with a litany of incidents that I presume should mean something to me. The room remains white…yes I am insane.

Perhaps my future is contained in this room. Alone with these thoughts I continue to write. I will not accept the nonsense they are saying. It cannot be true.

I am not dead. Surely there has been a mistake. Insane yes. Dead no. I could recover my sanity. Death at last look was terminal. Ridiculous.

The voices continue. Maybe I have been captured by an alien race and am being brain washed. That's it!

It makes sense! I am not dead. They are lying to me. I will be strong and prevail, they will not break me!

The present drags on and the voices continue. I no longer look to the future. All I have is now. In that thought process I notice the floor begin to turn a light blue color. The voices speak of acceptance and my ability to have it (death) on my terms. I wish they would stop speaking of death. I do not feel dead. In fact I feel pretty good.

Part of me desires surrender, the other belligerent in acceptance of my end. It occurs to me though if I were dead in my comprehension of death I would not be experiencing this environment. I would not be writing on this wall of stone. The white walls begin to take on a pattern. I turn frantically to the door awaiting my demise. Oddly the door opens easily. The voices become figures. I suddenly recognize who they are. They are my parents. I thought they were dead! They embrace me lovingly and I realize it was their voices I had heard for so long. Yes I am dead. But you know what death is? A transition to a new life. I hope someone reads this before they die. If you find yourself in a white room remember to listen carefully to the voices. They are probably someone you know.

Me

The Incredible Power Of Thought

Dear friend

I write from no where. Bizarre as it sounds this is true. Actually I am not really writing at all. My thoughts are forming images that you perceive as writing. Symbols of thought artistically painted so that you can design your own thoughts. Complicated yet so simple.

Now that we have established that I am writing let us now know why. It is in hopes that I will be able to warn you as to the incredible power of thought. Yes we have all heard the phrase "thought creates reality". On the physical level it is a catch phrase forcing one to accept responsibility for one's situation. Yet it is so much more than that. The power of a single thought sends ripples through space that interact with other ripples causing the fusion of all of them to form something that may have not been originally intended. Thus the ominous power of thought.

It is my intention to try to explain through my own experience where thought has brought me to. In my last physical shape I did not honor thought. It was taken for granted and not fully appreciated. I allowed thought to run rampant. It is not uncontrolled thought that is the problem it is misdirected thought and uniformed thought. In my case my thoughts of the ending of physical form consisted of nothing. I suppose it was fear that prevented me from doing so. Since there was no thought of my death thus there was no establishment of what was to come later. You see that is why I write from nothing. I created nothing through my lack of thought on the subject. Now to rectify the situation I must return to physical form to begin again. This time I will think of what I want in death. It is certainly not this.

Use thought wisely. Use it to create what you want. Intersect thought with positive. It is the only way. Take it from one who has viewed all the angles.

Me.

Sr. Mary Ellen 1934

Dear friend

I remember the bells chiming every morning before mass. The sun would barely peek over the horizon as we scuttled our way to chapel. The good sisters wrapped warmly in their wool capes filing rather rigidly through the cloister. There was always a hush as the doors closed and the grand organ began to play "Ave Marie". Those were my favorite moments. The setting somehow made me feel closer to God. In growing closer to God a postulant like my self would be that much closer to being a permanent servant of the Lord. I had wanted nothing more in my life.

My father was a farmer whose luck went from bad to worse. I had eight brothers and sisters and a mother worn from the travails of rural life and numerous pregnancies. When I turned fourteen it was easy to convince my father that I wanted to be a nun. His consent made me happy and lifted the responsibility of feeding me off of him.

Girls were not as useful as boys in running a farm. My father did not love me. I was merely a girl child and he did not really know what to do with me. My mother clouded with the endless drudgery of cooking, planting and cleaning barely noticed when we left for the convent.

I remember how crisp the air was on the wagon ride into town. I had my only dress and my best shoes on. Actually they were my only shoes and were given to me by a neighbor who had lost a girl to typhoid. They were rather large but I had stuffed them with hay before I left.

The parting with my father was abrupt. I do not remember if he even came inside with me. I don't think he did. The sister who greeted me was rather stern. I didn't expect a warm reception. I was in the house of God. My mission & purpose now was to serve God. I was taken to a small room and given a habit and white veil. One of the sisters cut my hair closely to my head. I was to begin orientation the following day. My cell was sparse but after sharing a bed with three sisters my whole life the privacy was a gift.

I spent the next 3 years studying the work of God. I took my final vows on a bleak February morning. My family did not attend.

I became a new person that day. I was a servant of God. My new name was Sr. Mary Ellen. The old Alison Louise no longer existed. I adapted well to religious life. I followed all the rules and became a teacher. I looked forward to my salvation & was dedicated to my faith.

I believed that by giving my self to Jesus that I was sure to be with him in heaven.

The years passed and I never left the convent. I prayed for the lost souls and gave assistance to the new postulants.

I remained a nun for 58 years. The church had taught me that a place was waiting for me at the hand of God. Jesus died to save our souls. I wished fervently that I could sacrifice myself as much as our Lord did.

The heart attack surprised me. I was walking through the cloister when a great pain seized my chest and knocked me to the floor. Gasping for air I reached for my rosary. I wanted to meet God in prayer. It was what I was taught. It was what I believed.

I surrendered without a fight. My lips whispering prayers of gratitude & humility. I tried to keep my eyes open so that I could see the gates of heaven. There was a great darkness but I could still feel my rosary between my fingers. I prayed as long as I could. Then it all became very silent.

I do not know how long I layed there. No one came through the cloister at that time of day. Perhaps I had somehow recovered. I tried to open my eyes. My senses were not cooperating. I did however hear a voice. It sounded like my father, which of course was impossible. He had been dead for years.

Finally I was able to open my eyes. I was still on the floor of the cloister. My father was hovering over me wiping my forehead with a cool cloth. He looked as he did when I was a child. The burden of life no longer emanated from his eyes. He looked relaxed. So relaxed that he almost appeared as someone else. It was the sound of his voice that verified who he was.

Tenderly he touched my face. I was surprised at his concern. I had no desire to embrace him. Our relationship had not been a loving one. I felt uncomfortable being so close to him. He started to speak but his mouth did not move. The words he spoke however were crystal clear. He said that he had been waiting for me. He regretted our relationship and the turn it had taken. He wanted me to know that fear and repression had turned him into someone he had regretted being. He apologized for not letting me know how much he loved me. I began to sob as he smiled tenderly & kissed my forehead. He had never ever kissed me. My heart felt a revival in its happiness.

He told me to return with my new awareness. Return? Where was I? Where was God and the gates of heaven? My father smiled and said "Look about you. You are there." In disbelief I looked around and only saw the cloister. Surely this was a cruel joke. My father touched my face and blended into the air. His last words were these. "Heaven is right there in your heart. The manifestation of gates and the like are not necessary if you are truly one with yourself. Now you are."

I recovered from my attack but kept my visit from my father tucked inside. I never told anyone because they would not have believed me. I know now that my father was right. I died peacefully in my sleep 5 years later. My father was indeed waiting for me because I had kept him in my heart. I decided to manifest the gates and all. Why not? God was amused.

Sr. Mary Ellen 1934

**

DeaR FRiEND

ANOTHER MOMENT IN ENDLESS TIME BRINGS
ME TO YOU A THOUGHT FOR YOU WHAT IF
MAN PERCEIVED Time as a line instead of a dot.
A dot with predestined parameters is not as
interesting as endless line. What decisions and
Philosophies would be different in your culture if that
were true

We came to tell you it is true. Our life choices would
have been dramatically different with this
information. We offer it as a gift. Make your
life meaningful. Take your time — there is an
eternity. We are there. Now you know. Make a
difference as we would have given this information.

Dear Friend

Another moment in endless time brings me to you.
A thought for you. What if man perceived time as a
line instead of a dot with predestined parameters. Is [it]
not as interesting as endless line. What decisions and

229

philosophies would be different in your culture if that were true.

We came to tell you it is true. Our life choices would have been dramatically different with this information. We offer it as a gift. Make your life meaningful. Take your time - there is an eternity. We are there. Now you know. Make a difference as we would have given this information.

**

Jeremiah Jackson

Dear friend

I do not know who you are. Your face blends with the heavens in a swirl of energy. In trying to focus on your face I become confused. In that confusion my whereabouts suddenly becomes ambiguous. Therefore I will leave my focus upon you. It is necessary to grasp my surroundings. We base our reality on the significant milestones of physical we perceive. I know no other way to verify my existence. Am I not existent without something exterior to verify my being?

The confusion subsides I can feel the surrounding space. I am altered therefore I must have died. The exact details escape me. However it was unscheduled and not immediately anticipated. Perhaps an accident? I do not recall.

I found this vehicle of communication quite by accident. Stumbling through corridors of others like my self I found a way to communicate. I am not sure who is hearing this dissertation. Perhaps no one. The exercise itself gives me comfort as I adjust. If no one hears it is all the same.

There are levels of understanding. I pass silently through them while writing. It is quite puzzling to simultaneously be doing two things at once. There are others who are like in manner. The dual participation is becoming easier. Who knows? Perhaps later I will be able to partake of more actions at once.

The limitations of the physical are becoming clearer. The blend of me becoming more blended in the scheme of things. If someone had attempted explanation before this my confusion would have been enormous.

Choices confront me. I am not pressured to make one I just do. In each decision I find myself becoming more powerful. The anticipation of those decisions is enticing. I am yearning for more. The whisper of growth penetrates my thoughts. It is like an elixir of pleasure.

It is almost to the moment where this communication will cease to be of value. I have evolved to a new manner of thought. Grateful and humble I bid you adieu. This has stabilized me in my new life, hopefully the same impact will apply to you.

Jeremiah Jackson

Samuels

Dear friend

Upon death I fully expected to stare in the face of God. To understand the mysteries of our universe while conversing with the creator of all things. I wanted to know if the Bible was fact, fiction or a collection of both. I wanted to know who Jesus Christ really was. I wanted to know if I ever really had another shot at life through reincarnation. There were many questions with just as many answers.

Imagine my surprise at the moment of transition. The only heavenly trumpets were a slight ringing in my ears. It became slightly annoying until it moved into a silence. My eyes as I knew them no longer existed. There was a sensing with out definition. Physical form represents boundaries. Spirituality has no definition. The edges spread outward from the soul beyond anything one can imagine.

I found myself relying on old physical patterns to define what was happening. Now I realize that it would have been much easier to accept the new ways. The ride to oblivion would have been smoother.

Do not become frightened by the term oblivion. It is merely a state of being. There is not an annihilation attached to it. It is just different.

Let us get back to the face of God. Obsessed with the concept I searched for an explanation. The lessons taught to me told of a confrontation with God. Where was it? I was alone.

Eons seemed to pass. There was nothing. Fear that everything had been a lie engulfed me. Betrayed by my race + culture I huddled alone without the face of God. Who had I prayed to all those years? Was it a mere fantasy? Was I that easily duped.

Surely there would be someone to comfort me. Where were all the angels + saints? Where was the mass consciousness? I was alone.

In my self pity I began to cry. The last time I had such an emotional display had been when I was ten years old at my mother's funeral. The tears dripped off my face + formed a tiny puddle just within my eyesight. The puddle glistened when I was able to focus between sobs. In a brief moment I caught a reflection of who I used to be in the puddle. It brought back many memories of my life. I noticed how much I had changed. There was more definition to my features. In fact I looked many years younger.

The image of me began to make its way through various scenarios + encounters in my life. As I viewed them I felt better. Too bad God was not here to see what a good life I had led.

My pride at a job well done filled me. Well if God was not around I would give myself absolution and be done with it. In fact I would create my own pearly gates of heaven.

No sooner than the thought came the gates of heaven materialized before me. Were they there before and I just did not see?

Impossible.

Two forms moved toward me. They appeared somewhat angelic but not what I expected. They appeared to have purpose as they strode up to me.

I asked the whereabouts of God. Puzzled they looked at each other than back to me. "God is here. You have just been in contact since you arrived. Did you not know?"

Of course these two were of no help. I had not been with anyone. I was alone.

The two beings then nodded knowingly. "My dear you are the presence of God as are we. God exists in all. You only needed to look inside to find him. Your tears were the windows. God has stared himself in the face and is pleased. You were never alone. You were with God."

In retrospect I probably should have been upset. However, the revelation hit me square between the eyes and I broke into laughter.

The enigma was way too simple. In my enlightenment the gates of heaven opened before me and I walked through. The face of God glistened before me in my own tears. The Face was my own. I get it.

Samuels

Gilbert B. Strothberg

DEAR FRIEND

I WEEP FOR THE MOMENT FOREVER UNLIVED. I WEEP FOR THE MEMORIES TUCKED CLOSELY INSIDE. MOSTLY I WEEP FOR YOU, THE ONE TO DECIPHER WHAT IS LEFT.

MY DEATH UNTIMELY, THE DETAILS IRRELEVANT. WHAT AWAITS THOSE WHO PASS OVER IS TRULY DIVINE. REGRETS REMAIN ONLY FOR YOU.

UNDERSTANDING A LIFE PATH IS NOT EASY. SO INDIVIDUAL THAT ANOTHER MAY NOT EVEN KNOW WHERE TO BEGIN. YOU ARE LEFT WITH THE "WHY". THE ANSWER IS IN ME BUT LEFT UNSAID WITHOUT THE PHYSICAL TO DELIVER. I HAVE SEARCHED FOREVER AND FOUND THIS PORTAL. I AM SUBLIMELY HAPPY. NOW I GIVE YOU A REASON TO BE AT PEACE. THE PHYSICAL SO FLEETING, THE SPIRITUAL ETERNAL. THE GAP BETWEEN WIDENED BY MERE COMMUNICATION.

I NO LONGER WEEP FOR NOW YOU ARE INFORMED. THE "WHY" TURNING TO UNDERSTANDING. IT WAS BECAUSE YOU FEEL FORGOTTEN + ALONE. KNOW THAT I HAVE NOT FORGOTTEN. ON THE CONTRARY I PREPARE A PLACE. THIS KNOWLEDGE SHOULD FORTIFY YOU.

DEATH BEGINS, NOT ENDS. WEEP NO LONGER. MOVE FORWARD TO A NEW LEVEL. ONE THAT DOES NOT REQUIRE PHYSICAL PRESENCE. A SPIRITUAL ONE IS ALL THAT IS REQUIRED.

YOU CAN UNDERSTAND IF YOU LOOK AT A BROADER PICTURE. THE SMALL PICTURE IS IRRELEVANT.

WE WEEP NO LONGER. NEITHER SHOULD YOU. REUNION IS AT HAND. REJOICE.

SINCERELY,

GILBERT B. STROTHBERG

DEAR FRIEND

   I WEEP FOR THE MOMENT FOREVER UNLIVED.
I WEEP FOR THE MEMORIES TUCKED CLOSELY INSIDE.
MOSTLY I WEEP FOR YOU, THE ONE LEFT TO DECIPHE,
WHAT IS LEFT.

   MY DEATH UNTIMELY, THE DETAILS IRRELEVANT.
WHAT AWAITS THOSE WHO PASS OVER IS TRULY
DIVINE. REGRETS REMAIN ONLY FOR YOU.

...

YOU CAN UNDERSTAND IF YOU LOOK AT A BROADER
PICTURE. THE SMALL PICTURE IS IRRELEVANT.

   WE WEEP NO LONGER. NEITHER SHOULD YOU.
REUNION IS AT HAND. REJOICE.

SINCERELY

GILBERT. B. STROTHBERG

Gerald

Dear Friend

So sorry to intrude. However the moment was ripe and I pluck the fruit from the vine. Never one to tarry with right amount of gossip. I now step forward to speak my mind. My name is Gerald Comstock Whitington III I am a rather dead person in your eyes, however I am alive and well, living in a void of reality that you would most likely call Limbo. At least that is, what we were told as children. I have waited for a moment and eternity to speak to someone, anyone who could hear me. No one does you know. Only this hand is accessible and it is selective. Patience not being my forte the mingling is difficult at best. You wonder why we write? We wonder why we would not. The opportunity so defined by this parchment. It gives me joy to communicate with you. No one has heard me til now. I am here. I am in the doorway as you step outside, I am amongst the flowers you smell, I am in the eyes of your children & pets. Merely trying to find a way to speak. At last at last At last.

My life so remarkable only to myself ended abruptly on a boating trip. I was gifted and lived a life of priveledge. Having forgotten other times this life swallowed up my essence and I became besotted with my own ego. Truly taken with the form presented to me. I did not appreciate priveledge. I expected it. Becoming godlike in my own small self view I became a creature of malice. In my ignorance I compiled quite a bit of debt. Karmic debt. What a fool.

I was devastated to find myself dead. There was no hope of reprieve. My poor body mutilated by a boat motor was a stunning likeness to my own inner self. I never got a good look at it until I was out of it. Perhaps if I had only taken the time to look. Then again I never would have as long as I was physical. Time is endless especially when no one hears you and one becomes anonomous to the cosmos. The lonliness of separation from the Source is indescribable. God exists as you and you are cut off from all including God. It is cosmic suicide. Regretting is not the same as recreating. To be sorry is not enough. Atonement through experience

heals more thoroughly. I now understand the path I must take. Thank you for listening. It is a great gift. Tend to your self, the inner, the higher and the one that experiences life. Do not wait until you are gazing from afar to see what it creates. If you find you are lacking take steps to atone. The universe is you and the universe if forgiving. I am dead but thanks to you no longer alone.

Gerald

242

Gerald

Dear Friend

So sorry to intrude. However the moment was ripe and I pluck the fruit from the vine. Never one to tarry with right amount of gossip I now step forward to speak my mind. My name is Gerald Comstock Whittington III. I am a rather dead person in your eyes however I am alive and well, living in a mode of reality that you would most likely call Limbo. At least that is what we were told as children. I have waited for a moment and Eternity to speak to someone, anyone who could hear me. No one does you know. Only this hand is accessible and it is selective. Patience not being my favorite the mingling is difficult at best. You wonder why we write? We wonder why we would not. The opportunity so defined by this parchment. It gives me joy to communicate with you. No one has heard me till now. I am here. I am in the doorway as you step outside. I am amongst the flowers you smell. I am in the eyes of your children & pets. Merely trying to find a way to speak. At last at last at last.

My life so remarkable only to myself ended abruptly on a boating trip. I was gifted and lived a life of privilege. Having forgotten other times this life swallowed up my essence and I became besotted with my own ego. Truly taken with the form presented to me. I did not appreciate privilege. I expected it. Becoming godlike in my own small self view I became a creature of malice. In my ignorance I compiled quite a bit of debt. Karmic debt. What a fool.

I was devastated to find myself dead. There was no hope of reprieve. My poor body mutilated by a boat motor was a stunning likeness to my own inner self. I never got a good look at it until I was out of it. Perhaps if I had only taken the time to look. Then again I would never have as long as I was physical. Time is endless especially when no one hears you and one becomes anonymous to the cosmos. The loneliness of separation from the source is indescribable. God exists as you and you are cut off from all including God. It is cosmic suicide. Regretting is not the same as recreating. To be sorry is not enough. Atonement through experience

243

heals more thoroughly. I now understand the path I must take. Thank you for listening. It is a great gift. Tend to yourself, the inner, the higher and the one that experiences life. Do not wait until you are gazing from afar to see what it creates. If you find you are lacking take steps to atone. The universe is you and the universe is forgiving. I am dead but thanks to you no longer alone.

Gerald

Sylvia

I sit on the edge of a paper moon.

My legs dangling into nothingness.

As far as the eye can see are stars of many facets.

Each angle a new regeneration of physical form as it reenters the other dimension.

I sit here engrossed at the vastness

of it all, hoping for clarity

in what it all means.

I've only sat here a brief while, my

death just another every day occurrence.

I wasn't special nor particularly talented.

The only people who knew me were those

of my small nowhere town.

Yet I sit here on the edge of a paper moon

in observance of all eternity.

The starry lights of all those who partake

of god and the universe give me comfort.

I am alone in the crowd but the crowd

comforts me for I am a part of all.

I sit on the edge of a paper moon.

My legs dangling into nothingness.

No one special am I.

I am god and the creator of all

the other stars confirm my thoughts.

The invitation is open for you when

you decide to come next to me on the

paper moon.

Or perhaps you'll create your own place

to sit. It's all up to you.

Sylvia

Mildred Bernstein Miller

Dear Friend

Whisper softly in your ear and still you don't hear me. The result of an energy shift so they tell me. I have pursued an avenue of communication for what seems like forever. The measurement of moments non existent while ever beating forward with you. So many doors closed in my face. Does no one feel my plight? Surely there have been others with the urgency to go back. Am I the only one? I have become a pilgrim searching for a new life of freedom where I can communicate as I will. No answers + most of all no acknowledgement cutting my heart to the quick. I can see my children crying for me while I wait here. Manacled to a here after which I am clearly not ready for. I stand silently beside them willing some notice some slight flicker of hope that they know I am here. So often brushing their cheek with my hand only to have them swipe the area as an insect bite. My heart aches that I can offer no comfort. And as they move on and put my painful absence aside, I see that they will survive. Torn between the joy of their strength + weakness of my loss, I wait.

The joy of this outlet has brought me comfort. The frustration of those caught in between with unresolved issues is truly the hell religion has spoke of. In other times I would have insisted upon a message to those I love. Now it is enough just to touch the physical again while purging my heart of what I have longed to do. It is difficult to pass quickly. No time to prepare, to say all the good things you planned on. Just a breath and you arrive unable to go back.

Thank you for this moment. I know now my children are safe and love me. I will be with them again. I am beginning to see a light in the distance. The self imposed silence has lifted. I move on also.

Thank you.

Mildred Bernstein Miller

Dear Friend

Whisper softly in your ear and still you don't hear me. The result of an energy shift so they tell me. I have pursued an avenue of communication for what seems like forever. The measurement of

...

Thank you for this moment. I know now my children are safe and love me. I will be with them again. I am beginning to see a light in the distance. The self imposed prison silence has lifted I move on also.

Thank you.

Mildred Berstein Miller.

Patrick Sindau

The darkness surrounds me. I am afraid. Beyond that which is me there is a void unexplored by human eyes. This void is like a small room where I retreat upon sleep and ultimately death. The dream envelops me briefly but I realize there will be a time where it envelops me completely and there will be no return. It scares me but I find bravery in the moment and I proceed to my destiny while in a dream.

My eyes open and the mist of the unreal recedes and I focus upon a room. It is small but vast and filled with crystals of every shape and size. I enjoy the energy of crystals and I revel in their existence in this self created dream state. I know I am dead and I know the significance of the crystals. They are records of the patterns of my past existences. If I hold one to my non existent temple I can relive that particular life. The dray of my existence recorded so sublimely in these crystals allows me to proceed to another level of life not known to me before. I am exuberant in this revelation. What a coup to review past projections to the level such as this. My respect for these receptacles has been minimal before this precise moment. A record of all that has transpired allows me to process my advancement. What a coup! A crystal holds the key to remembering. This room I am now manifesting my self is a record keeping receptacle of me. Please know whomever you are that these places exist for all. Yours is next to mine. This is why I am able to leave you this message. Your attraction is not minimal. There is purpose to it. There are so many lighted crystals about me. Some I recognize from my physical life. Some are new. They are holding everything I need to know. By holding them to my temple I am able to remember past lessons.

Death has become a blur. Now I exist with the receptacles of me. The crystals are surrounding me. They caress my soul and give me comfort as they will you.

I am finished. I will attempt another moment with you at another time. The crystals are full of energy. Energy stored from you. Do not ever destroy or misplace one.

We go now. The moment has drawn to a close.

Adieu

Patrick Sindau

　　　a fellow traveler.

Kasnar of Sobul

Dear friend

Now I sit upon a ledge that overlooks my life. Each nuance repeated before me in minute detail. Every moment a punctuation of my growth or lack of it. Now in the viewing I see the significance of the whole and the benefit of each moment as it contributes. An awesome vision at the least.

I am but a fragment of an entire universe. My deeds so important in physical remain so in the spiritual. To my surprise the most common gesture an important cog in the wheel. The moments least remembered are the ones to cause retrospection now. I had the potential of my actions reversed. Now it is crystal clear. Now I see the benefit of a noble moment. Physical manifestations are but an off shoot of the true energy of the soul. All is so unimportant but the nobility of the soul. Now I sit here wondering where I will find salvation. Will I evolve the way my soul has dreamed? Or will I close my eyes to the truth and sleep through another existence only to find myself again unfulfilled in the afterlife.

Nay I say. I will capture all that is good and noble. To remain in the light is my ultimate goal. My only misuse of the life spent would be not to remember per these lessons learned. I close my eyes to punctuate the dream and to write it into my soul imprint. If I am free I will remind myself of the importance of dreaming while physical. This remembrance will enhance my next physical moment and I will rocket out of body to the top of the cosmos for reunion.

You ask who I meet? It is the others. The others sent from my source to experience simultaneously this universe this vast adventure created by those like myself. I close the pages of my soul journal now to reenter the dream I have created. The evolution of all that is me has benefited from the contact. The vast arena of my being now leaping into oblivion rejoicing in the fact that you know I exist.

Expand your being. Become one with the others you know are there. It is time. A time of love and reunion.

We are delighted to blend with you.

Kasnar of Sobul

Dear friend
  Now I sit upon a ledge that overlooks my life
Each nuance repeated, before me in minute detail

Kaspar of Sobul

Stanley J. Patterson 1888

Dear friend,

The path to heaven is a mysterious one. In my lifetime I spent countless hours buried in scripture + behavior befitting an apostle of God. Instructed by my chosen religion I guided my self through various loopholes of Spirituality. Upon my death I found that all my preparations seemed to be in vain. All the trappings of heaven somehow alluded me. Where were the Pearly Gates? Where was St. Peter with his list of the chosen? My first glimpse of the hereafter was filled with clutter. In my misgivings of my destination I found my self surrounded by the barbaric replicas of my previous lives. Not remembering certain objects I immediately cried foul. After retrospection the clutter began to take shape and the events of past lives began to take shape. All of them intertwined towards a common goal. The path to heaven. It seems I have searched for it since the beginning of time.

Becoming more lucid in my post life state I began to explore. The walls were barren as long as I perceived them so. When I imagined certain settings they materialized fully before me. That took some getting used to. The immediate gratification of thoughts is something we all have forgotten in the physical.

I was obviously raised many times as a Christian. Arrogant in the teachings I always imagined the way of Jesus as the only way. It was the path of God. Or so I thought. Now in my continuing journey to heaven in the Spiritual I have encountered many travelers with this same goal. Oddly not all of them have the same presentations.

I know there is a heaven and I now see my self on the path. Therefore it is so. You see death does not guarantee a place in the heavens. The journey continues with a different agenda. I continue as you will when the time is right. Perhaps I shall wait for you to join my perspective with yours. I am told joint realities are more powerful. I'll think it over while I wait.

The path to heaven awaits us all.

Stanley J. Patterson 1888

Patrick O Murphy. 1974

Dear friend.

The wall feels cold as my finger tips brush across the surface. The tiny piece of rock scraping out these words is dwindling in size. Soon there will be none left. The message I leave is important only to myself. There is no possibility of light at the end of this tunnel. I have been here so long that memories of another place now seem like distant dreams. The idea of being here forever used to disturb me. Now in acceptance I leave this epitaph, scratched on the wall. It feels primitive in an odd sort of way. Perhaps this is how prehistoric man felt during the ice age. The thought gives me something to ponder so that I may not go mad.

You may wonder how I got here. It was a winding path to be sure. I was successful. A man of means. College grad, and a social climber. Always ready to better my "future" any way I could. In retrospect I played dirty but I was always compensated with material objects. If it feels good do it. A man who had everything but honor. I always figured there would be time to make amends with God or whoever at the end. It could wait till I was ready. I had plenty of time, a lot to do. That is until I stumbled off the curb into an oncoming bus. My last thought was about the meeting I was now going to be late for.

Since then it's been me and these cold stone walls. A reflection I'm told of who I am. Pretty grim.

If any one ever follows me here (and I'm sure I could give you a few names) perhaps they will read my message. It would be better to read it before but I'm doubtful it could cross back over. This will just have to do. I was wrong. So wrong. The nourishment of the soul is vastly more important than the abundance of material. I wish I had another chance to try again. I'm told there will be. I've yet to understand what the meaning of that is. If I get another chance I will be more spiritually informed.

Believe me.

Patrick O Murphy. 1974

Dear friend,
The wall feels cold as my fingertips brush across the surface. The tiny piece of rock scraping out these

...

had another chance to try again. I'm told there will be. I've yet to understand what the meaning of that is. If I get another chance I will be more spiritually informed. Believe me,

Patrick Q Murphy. 1974

SABAN

Dear friend,

I sat today pondering the universe. I sat on the edge of a crescent moon created by my own thoughts. I like the latter part the best. The part where my thoughts materialize with a mere intake of breath. I can remember being told while physical that I could create any thing I wanted. Of course the concept seemed like bull to me at the time. I didn't realize that while solid creation sometimes takes more force of thought and time, my impatience acted like a deterrent stopping or further delaying the process. Impatience being a negative.

So now while spiritual I get the idea. My goal would be to remember this when starting a new physical life. In this state there are many ideas worth remembering. However it doesn't always work that way. I wanted to let someone know that I am returning. There are a few items I'd like to experience. You would ask how many times I have lived. You know I cannot remember them all. Can you recall the details of everyday of your present life? Of course not. Only important events stand out. It is the same for myself.

260

Certain episodes are very clear while others are faded or simply non existent.

I have yet to meet God or anything that might resemble him. Raised many times in structured religion I find it hasn't' applied yet. The energy of my thoughts vibrate about me, as do the thoughts of others who are here. The blending of those pure energies does create a heaven of sorts. All the stories I was taught seem to be simply that...stories.

So I sit here on a crescent moon. My legs dangle among the stars and I am writing. This letter may never go beyond this moment however it doesn't matter. By merely thinking of its delivery I am sure it is done in some fashion. I bid whoever you are a great forever. When you come here look for me. A crescent moon isn't hard to find. Hopefully I'll be here in that moment. If not wait for me, the physical is so fleeting. I would return in a moment.

SABAN

Samuel Peterson

Dear friend

At last a window! Hope was all I had left upon departure. Ever ready for adventure this time the fear of the truly unknown overpowered me. I was not able to bring anything of comfort with me. As all comfort had manifested itself in a physical world. Thus hope came along. The initial panic of physical loss was almost unbearable. So intertwined with the body I had forgotten any other type of existence. I wanted to open my eyes but realized the stupidity of it. No longer did I have eyes. I strained to listen for any minute sound but alas I had no ears. I tried to call out but again I had no mouth. In my struggle to adapt I clung to hope, more than I had while physical. Without it surely I would have perished. I became aware through my spiritual senses. It was more comfortable to suppose I still had my body, so I created it. It was comfortable to super impose my expectations upon my surrounding. It gave me time to adjust. Spiritual existence is more ancient than physical and therefore more finely turned. Each thought is a spring board to fulfillment. To have only five senses now seems so simple and primitive. Hope has flourished inside me and the possibilities are limitless. I write so that others may take this knowledge with them. Perchance hope will lead to further enlightenment. I have expanded so thoroughly the possibility of return to physical seems unfulfilling. How silly to fear it. I would have benefited from knowledge such as this but then again my relationship with hope would have floundered. All is as it should be. I am so pleased to have this moment. It is a co-creation, which is necessary to connect between the two places.

The window begins to close as I open to more possibilities. The expansion is a marvel and a gift.

We bid you farewell.

Samuel Peterson

Dear friend

At last a window! Hope was all I had left upon departure. Ever ready for adventure this time the fear of the truly unknown overpowered me.

...

The window begins to close as I open to more possibilities. The expansion is a morsel and a gift.

We see you farewell.

Samuel P. Kish

Daniel

DEAR FRIEND

THE MOMENTS DURING THE LAST DAY ARE FILLED WITH FEAR. AS IN ALL DRAMAS THE CURTAIN MUST EVENTUALLY GO DOWN. THE FINAL DIALOGUE ALWAYS UN REHEARSED AND MOST OFTEN UN FULFILLING. I RECALL ANTICIPATION MIXED WITH REGRET. I SO ENJOYED PHYSICAL EXISTENCE. THAT LIFE IN PARTICULAR SO FILLED WITH SOUL ATTACHMENTS. IT WAS NOT OFTEN THAT I WAS INCARNATED WITH SO MANY. SO IN THOSE LAST MOMENTS GOODBYES SO FINAL WERE ABUNDANT. IT WOULD BE MANY LIVES BEFORE WE WERE TO BE REUNITED. THE SADNESS MOST UNBEARABLE. HOWEVER THE LAST BREATH WAS NOT AS PAINFUL AS I PROJECTED. IT WAS LIKE HOLDING ONE'S BREATH AND REALIZING THAT AN ADDITIONAL ONE WAS NOT NECESSARY. I DID HAVE A VERY BRIEF MOMENT OF PANIC. IT WAS NOT LONG. I THOUGHT TO OPEN MY EYES AND REALIZED THAT THERE WAS NO

NEED. NOW IN A MOMENT OF REFLECTION I FIND THIS SPACE. THIS SPACE AWAITING MY HAND. AT FIRST I WAS TIMID. THUS FINDING MYSELF "BUMPED" OUT OF LINE. THERE ARE OTHER DENSITIES OF LIFE ALSO DESIRING A VOICE. MUCH TO MY SURPRISE. SO I WAITED FOR ANOTHER OPPORTUNITY, AND IT HAS ARRIVED. MY MESSAGE, SO SIMPLE. "I AM HERE". I OCCUPY THE SAME SPACE ONLY WITH LESS DENSITY. AS YOU WILL.

THAT IS ALL. I STEP ASIDE TO PROVIDE OTHERS A MOMENT. NO NEED TO SEND MOMENTOS TO THOSE STILL LIVING. IT WOULD NOT SERVE THEM.

DANIEL

(Note that this letter was hand printed in all upper case letters.)

DEAR FRIEND

THE MOMENTS DURING THE LAST DAY ARE FILLED WITH FEAR. AS IN ALL DRAMAS THE CURTAIN MUST EVENTUALLY GO DOWN.

...

THAT IS ALL I STEP ASIDE TO PROVIDE OTHERS A MOMENT. NO NEED TO SEND MOMENTOS TO THOSE STILL LIVING. IT WOULD NOT SERVE THEM

DANIEL

Benjamin Wyatt Watkins

DEAR FRIEND

I SENSE YOUR SADNESS. IT PREVENTS MY ASSIMILATION TO A NEW LEVEL OF BEING. WHY DO YOU WEEP SO? IS IT MY DEPARTURE OR YOUR SENSE OF LOSS? REALIZE THERE WAS NO DISCOMFORT FOR ME. IN FACT THE SHEDDING OF THE PHYSICAL FORM WAS INVIGORATING. IMAGINE TOTAL FREEDOM FROM THE CONSTRAINTS OF BIOLOGY. MY THOUGHTS MORE PURE THEREFORE MORE POWERFUL. THE EMANCIPATION OF THIS MOMENT IS WELL CHERISHED. I BESEECH YOU TO CEASE WEEPING AND TO PLOT YOUR OWN COURSE TO ELEVATION. TRULY I FEEL MORE CONNECTED TO YOU AND THE UNIVERSE NOW. YOUR TEARS MERELY HINDER MY FOCUS. YOU WILL UNDERSTAND WHEN YOU HAVE EVOLVED TO THIS STATE. UNTIL THEN ALL YOU REALLY HAVE IS MY WORD. 'TIS THE REASON FOR MY COMMUNICATION. YOUR VALUE OF MY WORD. THERE HAVE BEEN MANY TO COMMUNICATE AND EVEN MORE WHO SEEK A PORTAL. THERE ARE FEW REAL ONES. THIS ONE IS TRUE. IF WE HAD PONDERED DEATH MAYBE WE COULD HAVE ESTABLISHED A SIGNAL. HOWEVER LIFE BEING WHAT IT IS THERE WAS NO OPPORTUNITY. WE

WERE MORE INVOLVED IN LIFE THAN DEATH. NOW IT IS YOUR TIME TO BE INVOLVED AS AN AID IN LIFE. IT IS ESSENTIAL TO YOUR PROCESS. IF YOU CEASE TO LIVE FULLY WE MAY NEVER MEET. NOT TO SCARE YOU. ONLY TO COAX YOU INTO THE REALIZATION THAT YOU MUST BE IN THE PROPER PLACE ENERGETICALLY. I LEFT IN FULL LIFE GEAR. YOU MUST DO THE SAME SO THAT THE VIBRATION OF OUR ENERGIES MATCH. TO BE DEAD WHILE ALIVE WILL ONLY MISLEAD YOU TO A DIFFERENT PLACE. NOT ONE WHERE I WOULD BE ABLE TO EMBRACE YOU. THINK + UNDERSTAND FULLY. THIS IS SOUND ADVICE.

THE PROCESS IS INDEED COMPLEX. BUT I HAVE EXPERIENCED IT. THERE ARE MANY MORE LEVELS. I LOOK FORWARD TO THEM. LIVE AND BE ACTIVE. MY SPIRIT IS WITH YOU! THIS MOMENT TO SHARE COMES BUT ONCE. I MUST MAKE WAY FOR OTHER VOICES.

I AWAIT YOU. LIVE!

BENJAMIN WYATT WATKINS

(Note that this letter was hand printed in all upper case letters.)

Dear Friend

I sense your sadness. It prevents my assimilation to a new level of being. Why do you weep so? Is it my departure or your sense of loss? Realize there was no discomfort for me; in fact the shedding of the physical form was envigorating. Imagine total freedom from the

...

The process is indeed complex but I have experienced it. There are many more levels, I look forward to them. Live and be active. My spirit with you! This moment to share comes but once. I must make way for other voices.

I await you. Live!

Benjamin Wyeth Watkins

Jared

Dear friend

It seems a moment ago I was among the flesh. I remember counting moments. Each one a milestone of sorts. The measurement of existence, the pulse of a minute and the rapid grouping into hours, days, months, and years. I remember the significance and the detail of every drama span. Oh how important it all seemed. Preoccupation with quantity out numbering the jubilation of quality. Somehow the point missed severely by this self. Yes I remember. Perhaps a ponderance such as the one I experience now will enhance future physical endeavors. A slowing of the living pace that has blurred the real depth of life. I have no regrets only the desire to relive the choices I made.

The opportunity to share is a miracle. The walls of separation between these two states of existence so thick. The mere frustration of not being heard rings soundly through my essence. Surely the heavens have pled mercy for me. The solemn quite here allows for transition to a higher standard. I would have never realized this level of growth while physical. I was too busy measuring time and lamenting at the lack of it.

Each moment should be savored. A sensual experience so sublime it defies definition. Physical existence is a gift, not an accident. Evolution of the soul requires a full immersion into the flesh.

I ponder now why it was so muddled while there. The opportunity to return has not presented itself yet. Only this small opening to a writing tablet + pen. One must be grateful for what one is given. Hopefully this note will reach someone with the same perception as I. And perhaps, just perhaps it will open the door for that individual to realize what is important. For that I am grateful.

I await the next opportunity. Be blessed and live. Appreciate the quality. Be not obsessed with the quantity.

Jared

Louise

Dear friend

I always loved the seasons of the year. Each one held its place in my heart. I did not have a favorite. The rotation of events was always an inspiration to me. Major passings in my physical life were always marked by the seasons. I was born in the spring. I grew up in the fall. I married in the summer. My first child borne in the winter. There are many more but time is limited for this endeavor. My death was planned. That may sound macabre but I knew I was ill and decided that I wanted to die in the winter. I could not have endured a death in spring. So on a snowy day in January I made my departure. There were no regrets. It was my time. My last breath was crisp and cold. All faded away until I was the last thing in the universe. I purposely tried to stay alert. I wanted to know where I was going. Where ever that was. I had learned all the Sunday school stories and was now ready to see if they were all true. And I waited. Everything was white. No definition. I moved my gaze to every angle I thought of. My perception felt off because of the blazing white nothingness. For a while it felt anti climatic. Was this all there was?

In an effort to distract myself I began to think about the tulip bulbs I planted in the fall. I hoped that someone would view their splendor in the spring. They were my favorites. My thoughts began to appear before my eyes. The tulips in their multi splendor began to grow before my eyes. On the white background they were magnificent. As they grew they multiplied until my whole vision was filled with flowers. They were more than alive. They had consciousness. Whispering endearments as they intertwined with what I felt was my soul. This was a heavenly spring and it was only the beginning. I was to experience my beloved seasons on a new level of existence. So this was truly heaven. I can hardly wait for summer, autumn, + winter.

I am glad for the opportunity to record this experience. Truly a gift.

Louise

Dear friend
    I always loved the seasons of the year. Each one held its place in my heart. I did not have a favorite. The rotation of events was

...

I am glad for the opportunity to record this experience. Truly a gift

Louise

Jasper

DEAR FRIEND

THIS IS NOT WHAT I EXPECTED. THERE IS
NOTHING THAT APPEARS TO BE SOLID.
SUNDAY SCHOOL CLASSES NEVER FORETOLD
A PLACE SUCH AS THIS. THERE ARE WALLS
THAT ARE RATHER FLIMSY. SO MUCH THAT
THEY ARE ALMOST NON EXISTENT. IF I
CONCENTRATE THEY BECOME MORE SOLID.
MORE FOCUS PROVIDES A COOLER HUE. IT IS
INTERESTING THAT THE CHANGES OCCUR
WITH INTENSITY OF THOUGHT. I WONDER
WHERE HEAVEN IS. SURELY IT EXISTS. WHY
WERE WE TOLD OF SUCH A PLACE IF IT DOES
NOT EXIST. I LIVED A GOOD LIFE. WHY AM I
NOT THERE?

I AM SITTING ON WHAT APPEARS TO BE A
FLOOR. THERE IS STILL NOTHING. I WISH I
COULD COMMUNICATE WITH MY BROTHER.
HE WAS AT MY SIDE WHEN I DIED. I CAN
STILL FEEL HIS HAND IN MINE. THE FINAL
MOMENTS WERE CALM AND THEN MY FOCUS
CHANGED TO HERE. IS THERE NO ONE TO

GREET ME? I WAS TOLD THERE WOULD BE OTHERS.

IT IS HARD TO CALCULATE TIME. IT SEEMS BUT AN ENDLESS MOMENT. I WONDER IF THIS WILL REMAIN THIS WAY FOR ETERNITY. THERE IS NOTHING. TO AMUSE MYSELF I BEGIN TO HUM AN OLD BEATLES' SONG. AS THE MELODY ESCAPES ME THE WALLS BEGIN TO PULSATE. THE THOUGHTS I AM HAVING ARE MANIFESTING THEMSELVES LIKE A HOME MOVIE. PERHAPS IF I IMAGINE MY SELF ALIVE IT WILL HAPPEN. AS I CLOSE MY EYES I FEEL A PHYSICAL SENSATION. MY OLD BODY IS BEFORE ME. AS I GAZE UPON IT, IT FADES AWAY. I FEEL SORRY BUT I LET IT GO IN PEACE.

I'M GETTING THE IDEA OF MY NEW HOME. WHATEVER I THINK BECOMES REALITY. THE EMPTY SPACE NOW HAS DEPTH. AS I WRITE THESE THOUGHTS I AM BECOMING AWARE OF OTHERS. IT IS NOT WHAT I EXPECTED OF COURSE. ONE CANNOT CREATE WITH ONLY EXPECTATION, ONE NEEDS TO CREATE WITH BELIEF. SUNDAY SCHOOL ONLY TAUGHT THE END RESULT. ONE HAS TO CREATE THE

HEREAFTER. IT IS SO PERSONAL. NOT UNIVERSAL. I FEEL BETTER NOW. HOPEFULLY SOMEONE WILL READ THIS.

JASPER

DEAR FRIEND
THIS IS NOT WHAT I EXPECTED.
THERE IS NOTHING THAT APPEARS TO BE
SOLID. SUNDAY SCHOOL CLASSES NEVER
FORTOLD A PLACE SUCH AS THIS. THERE ARE

...

BELIEF. SUNDAY SCHOOL ONLY
END RESULT. ONE HAS TO CREATE THE
HEREAFTER. IT IS SO PERSONAL NOT UNIVERSAL
I FEEL BETER NOW. HOPEFULLY SOMEONE WILL
READ THIS

Jasper.

Sarah Jean T Maxwell

Dear friend

A chance to change the path of a life is such an opportune thing. I sit alone gazing at all the lives pulsing before me and I wonder. Are they all important? Does each one have a special impact upon the rhythm of the universe? I never thought of these things while physical. The mundane drama of everyday issues kept my focus pretty muddled. Now in the light I see more clearly. By focusing on one dot of energy I find its life pattern manifesting itself before me. Should I intervene? The opportunity surely exists. The acceptance of such an intrusion is doubtful. However my goals are now different. So I write this letter to that one speck of light. Its energy becomes more pure by integrating with mine. I feel an absolute surge of energy so valuable I cannot define it.

Just the knowledge of an after life has altered the course of this soul. (I call them souls when viewed so intimately). The reading of script from the spiritual lends itself to salvation. I cry from the heavens that there is much more. By relating this to you my friend we become more.

Appreciate the moment. Evolve to the light. Read my letter and know. As energy multiplies it rises to the heavens and is saved. In this moment you have raised your vibration for all eternity. Continue. The path is long.

Sarah Jean T Maxwell

Amir

DEAR FRIEND

HOW DIFFERENT WOULD LIFE BE IF WE
WERE BOLD ENOUGH TO ENACT ALL OF OUR
THOUGHTS? IN LIFE I PONDERED THE
POSSIBILITIES OF WHAT I COULD DO. IT WAS
FAR DIFFERENT THAN WHAT I DID DO. DID
THAT MAKE ME A FAILURE? SHOULD I
REGRET THE INACTION'S MORE THAN SOME
OF THE ACTIONS? IN MY LAST MOMENTS I
WONDERED. DID I LIVE FULLY? DID I MISS
SOMETHING. WERE THERE REGRETS UPON
THE LAST BREATH? I DECIDED ONE MUST
LIVE BOLDLY. NOT WITH HIGH DRAMA
CONTENT BUT WITH CONVICTION OF
WHATEVER YOU DEEM TO BE IMPORTANT. IN
MY LIFE REVIEW I WATCHED MYSELF TIME +
TIME AGAIN STEP BACK FROM THE FLOW OF
ENERGY THAT WOULD HAVE ENABLED A
TRANSFERENCE TO A NEW LEVEL OF
UNDERSTANDING. WHY? IT WAS BECAUSE OF
MY FEAR OF ANY REPERCUSSION. THE
INABILITY TO SEE BEYOND THE MINUTE

MOMENT TO THE VAST UN COUNTABLE MOMENTS THAT WOULD HAVE LED TO A HIGHER STATE OF CONSCIOUSNESS. THUS MY LETTER NOW. IN HIND SIGHT I SEE THE PATH OFTEN MISSED BY MISPLACED FEAR, ARROGANCE, + DOWN RIGHT STUPIDITY. LIFE IS A GIFT. EACH MOMENT AN OPPORTUNITY TO EXPAND AND FLY TO THE HEAVENS. AND YES THERE IS ONE. NO, I RETRACT THAT. THERE ARE MANY. EACH MOMENT THERE IS OPPORTUNITY FOR GROWTH. IT ALL DEPENDS IF YOU ARE BOLD ENOUGH TO GRAB IT BEFORE IT PASSES YOU BY. AND IT WILL PASS YOU BY. NOW IN THE GLORIOUS MOMENTS OF AFTERLIFE I BREATHE THE CRYSTAL AIR + BECOME SOMEWHAT ANGELIC. MY ONLY DESIRE IS TO MAINTAIN THIS STATE UPON REENTRY FOR ANOTHER TRY. A TRY TO EVOLVE TO THE NEXT LEVEL. EXPANSION OF THE SOUL IS THE ULTIMATE EXPERIENCE. WE SUGGEST YOU DO NOT MISS IT.

AMIR

DEAR FRIEND
    HOW DIFFERENT WOULD LIFE BE IF WE WERE
BOLD ENOUGH TO ENACT ALL OF OUR THOUGHTS.?

...

TO EVOLVE TO THE NEXT LEVEL. EXPANSION OF THE
SOUL IS THE ULTIMATE EXPERIENCE. WE SUGGEST YOU
DO NOT MISS IT.

    AMIR

Myulla

Dear friend,

I see now the folly of my ways. The moments lost to senseless drama while my life lessons unfolded before me. Oh to have the veil of illusion lifted before the final call. To apply the energy toward what is most important. Physical issues intended to lead one to redemption becoming confused + confounded until the real intent is distorted. If one were able to simplify the enigma instead of compounding it there would be much growth. I managed to cling to my issues quite efficiently throughout physical. My ego enabling the malfunction of the process enough to allow a tail chasing effect to emerge. In retrospect I see the folly but in the moment paralyzed to do anything about it. It seems many lives are ended this way. I can name several of my own with endings as disappointing. My only hope is to render this moment to memory, cell memory at least. Therefore catapulting myself to a new level of understanding + definition. This moment of clarity comes only briefly between lives. I am thankful for the opportunity for this writing. I am hoping in my next level of existence that I will find my message. In

285

its assimilation I hope to find salvation from the spiral I have committed myself to.

Please if anyone finds this note, release it of definition of any kind. So that I may discover it and find my true self. For it is for certain that I create yet another spiral away from all that is. This note will serve my commitment to self realization. All I need to do is find it. Please help me. The process begins again. I am weary of the path. Let me discover who I am.

Thanks to anyone who listens.

Myulla

Mathilde

Dear friend

My last hours were spent in reflection on a life that I loved. Every moment a new idea which often led to a new adventure. I wanted so desperately to take it all with me. The creations so exquisite I dared not hope to ever achieve them again. So I met death with disappointment. Life was so great surely what was to come would pale in comparison. I found myself cursing my fate. If only there would be a few more moments to experience. A few more nuances to feel. Feeling cheated my eyes closed and in resignation I took my last breath.

The silence and darkness that greeted me were telling although I did not yet understand. Straining to see feel or hear anything I plunged deeper into despair. The emptiness engulfing me until I felt the real implosion of non existence. Weeping I again cursed the outside forces that had brought me to this. Ripping me away from all the creation I had loved. Down into the spiral I fell until the only sound I did hear were my sobs at the injustice of it all. Why did we have to die.

Racked with sorrow I suddenly realized that I could still cry. My sobs still could echo even when I knew that my physical body was no longer functional. How could this be? The silence and darkness continued but why should I care if I no longer existed. What defined existence? My reactions were proof enough to me. I began to think of my past life. As I did so images began to appear before me. My thoughts a tapestry woven through individual thought patterns. As I added a memory the scene before me strengthened and became clearer. With nothing else to do I began to fill all the darkness. Favorite melodies filled the silence. The silence + the darkness dimming in my presence until they no longer existed. I began to see clearly other beings like myself inside their own creations. As we blended our small universes it became a collage of color, sound and beauty.

My ability to create was beyond my expectations. This place, my universe was more beautiful than anything I had ever experienced. Truly a new lease on life. Different but equally exciting. And most importantly eternal. To be able to be here I had to shed the physical. It was nothing compared to this. Death is necessary for spiritual evolvement. We do not need our bodies to exist. Death is a timely process by which we realize our full potential. It is only dark + silent until we offer our souls and surrender. I no longer feel regret. Only appreciation of the process. I know that there are those who cling to physical even more vehemently than I. This is the reason for my communication, to tell you it's okay to let go.

What awaits you is spectacular if you only let it be so.

Mathilde

Dear friend,
My last hours were spent in reflection on a life that I loved. Every moment a new idea which often led to a new adventure. I wanted so desperately to take it all with me. The creations

...

What awaits you is spectacular if you only let it be so.
Mathilde

MATHILDE

HAGAR

Dear friend

An unusual display of affection filled my last moments of life. The extremeness of where I was and where I was going scared me. I desired to cling to that which was familiar and safe. Thus the embracement of people and things around me. Some would say it out of character for a rogue such as I. In fact I am in total agreement for it was fear that triggered the moment.

Now I remember most of the lives lived. There are a few that remain dim in exactness. However those of impact are at the fingertips of my soul memory.

Being of warrior essence my lives whether male or female all had the same tone of collision. An odd word I know but it describes the manner of the lives lived. I collided with just about everything. Conflict a drug of choice. It invigorated me and gave me purpose. Each little battle a prelude to my ultimate goal of conflict. It is how I learned my lessons. It filled me with pride to overcome, conquer and prevail. I know no other way. I see now there are varying points of view depending on your essence origins. To get back to my initial theme I must say that the moment of transition is frightful.

Even a warrior such as myself quivers at the thought of the unknown. However it is not unknown only forgotten. A quick warrior's death in the heat of battle so common to me was better than a more subdued battle with disease.

In my next attempt I shall script a more warrior like transition. Being fearful is so foreign to me. I suppose it was written for me to experience it. I write so that others not as brave as myself will make the transition easier.

My time for retrospection is about to end. I search for another opportunity for conflict. Or perhaps it would serve me better to recreate that lone display of affection. I still prepare so there is a moment to decide. Without that experience I never would be communicating with you in this way.

All has purpose including death. We bid you Godspeed.

HAGAR

Jessica

Dear friend;

It was a strange experience this dying. I knew it was coming. I was fearful yet resigned to the fact. Life was too short. I had enjoyed it immensely and I bemoaned the fact I was leaving my loved ones behind. I did not look forward to the "adventure". Surely all the hoopla about the Pearly Gates, Heaven and St. Peter were pure myth. They were created to take the fear out of the annihilation of it. The end. Game Over. I knew that. I was scared but scared doesn't matter when the end comes. It just comes and that is that.

I closed my eyes and fell asleep. Or so I thought. The dream began almost instantly. There I was in my backyard. Three years old and running through the sprinkler. A hot muggy day. The little T-shirt and pants I was wearing clung to me. The excitement when the sprinkler hit my body thrilled me to extremes. Screaming with joy I ran through one more time and surely that would not be the end. My backyard was the same as ever. Swing set, Sandbox, Dollhouse. An unending afternoon of sunshine and frivolity. I had had this dream before and suddenly I recalled that it indeed was a dream. There was something else to remember but it slipped my mind.

Little friends came over to play with me. Each of them participating with various games. Laughter and fun. It was all so pleasurable. I could do this forever. When I was a child I did not measure time. It just was. I had forgotten that.

The endless day was filled with friends and laughter. I caught my breath after another game of tag under the willow tree. I always liked it there. The sandbox around the base. The wind rippling through the branches. My favorite spot. There was a blue colored bird that used to sing there. I called him Blueberry. He just called me. Looking up I saw him. Gosh I had missed him. When I was five he told me many things.

Maybe he could help me remember what is so important. I look up and he begins to sing. His song filled with hope love + charity. Somehow it's different than when I was a child. I am becoming confused. Blueberry sits on my shoulder and comforts me. He tells me to remember. I cannot. He tells me to look up in the sky. I cannot. He tells me to look at my hands. I cannot. He tells me I'm dead. Not true. He tells me to fly with him. Can I?

Blueberry sits with me while I remember. I am dead. Is this just a dream? Or was living a dream? Blueberry says he'll be whatever I want him to be as will my death.

So I sit with him and we play in the sunshine Blueberry + me. For eternity. A place as close to heaven as I can imagine. And heaven is indeed what you imagine.

Jessica

Eric

Dear friend

I have stood in the shadows for so very long. The edges of darkness always at my fingertips. I have seen the sun and marveled at its magnificence. Having read all the philosophy of the human condition I settled for what could be mine and what couldn't be. So now it is the end of my existence, the shadows deepen about me. In my final moments I feel cheated. The brightness of living always quite close but always out of focus. How could I have been so wronged. Cursing the life force that now extracted itself from me I felt my lungs collapse for the last time. My anger at the injustice of it all came forth in a final attempt at life. Of course it was unsuccessful. The anger became part of my essence. A horrible sight to see once one is truly dead. It manifests itself before you rearing its ugly head. Its mocking tone telling you that it would have been better to release it in life.

I suddenly realize what the shadows have been trying to tell me. They existed only because I let them. How hard it is to face one's own creations. Especially when they are so negative. I feel ashamed. I now long for the opportunity to dispel the shadows and anger. This place of waiting where I currently exist holds a promise of salvation. I must return to turn the tide. Return to physical. It is something I never wished for but now feel a deep yearning. I close my eyes and slip into the shadows. I shall be reborn.

Eric

H

DEAR FRIEND

I AM THINKING. I HAVE BEEN THINKING FOR EONS. I FLOAT BETWEEN TWO HORIZONS. ONE WHISPERS OF LOVE LOST IN THE SHADOW OF A BODY. THE OTHER CLEARLY STATES THE IMPOSSIBLE WHILE BECKONING ME WITH OUTSTRETCHED ARMS. I AM TORN. THE DIRECTION OF MY FLIGHT ELUDES ME. I AM THINKING FOR I FEAR ANNIHILATION IF I SHOULD STOP.

THOUGHTS RAMBLE BETWEEN THE TWO HORIZONS. DO THEY EXIST BECAUSE OF ME? OR DO THEY EXIST IN SPITE OF ME? I CANNOT RECALL ANOTHER PLACE, PERHAPS I HAVE HOVERED HERE ETERNALLY. MY DESTINY POISED ON THE DECISION BETWEEN THE TWO HORIZONS.

THERE IS NO LIMIT ON THE TIMING OF MY DECISION. HOWEVER SOME TRYING PRODS ME TO HURRY ON MY WAY. AN INSTINCT SO PRIMAL I WONDER OF ITS ORIGIN.

WAS THERE MORE THAN THIS? I CANNOT RECALL. MY FOCUS BECOMES ONE WITH THE HORIZONS. A VERY SERIOUS CHOICE FLOATING, I THINK THE DECISION IS COMING. I AM FILLED WITH CONTENTMENT. I ATTEMPT TO LET FATE MAKE THE MOVE. I REALIZE THE FUTILITY OF THIS AND I DECIDE. THE OUTSTRETCHED ARMS OF IMPOSSIBILITY EMBRACE ME. I TURN FOR A FINAL GLIMPSE OF THE SHADOW. IT RELEASES ME WITH LOVE. I FEEL SAD FOR THE BODY LEFT BEHIND. IT HOWEVER KNOWS THE PROCESS AND RETURNS TO DUST TO BE BORN AGAIN.

I AM THINKING AND THE THOUGHT TURNS INTO A MELODY THAT I RIDE TO THE HORIZON. REALIZATION OF ETERNITY FILLS ME. I HAVE PASSED TO THIS NEW HORIZON. MY THOUGHTS MATERIALIZE BEFORE ME. I REMEMBER NOW THAT THIS IS CALLED DEATH. I AM THINKING AND IT IS WONDROUS.

H

(Note: This was letter was hand printed in all upper case.)

Gino

Dear friend

A pinpoint of energy beckons me to this spot. At least I believe it's a spot. Is it because I believe it therefore creating it or is it so because it has an energy source of its own. Or better yet does it exist because of the intersection of energies. I am confused. Ideas and emotions are milling about inside me. In some moments I feel about to explode. Others I feel shrinkage in my essence. I was not always in this state of being. There were moments just a breath ago where I was simply a cook in a greasy spoon restaurant in Queens NY. My biggest thought process of the day was getting out of bed and why I should. I moved through my life automatically. Sleep, Eat, Work, Play Sleep eat work play. My mantra since the age of 16. I quit school to make some money. Thinking was not my priority. Now I see that perhaps it should have been.

I did not understand the connection of thought and how it applied to my life. Sure I thought about things. You know like what to eat, where I wanted to go, things like that. On a primary level I thought things into reality. Never did I realize the enormity of the gift of thought.

Now I see this pinpoint of energy. I have thought about it. So now I have many questions. Of course no one is near to answer. I wish I had these questions while living. Speaking this out loud relieves some of the regret. Perhaps my voice will carry in some miraculous way and I will be heard. Thinking makes stuff happen. Knowing it early on makes all the difference.

Ginno

303

Mathew

Dear friend

I sit on the horizon. The sun envelopes me in its warmth and I become one in its energy. Swirling ever upward I feel the life force dictated by ancient gods swell inside of me. There is no longer a body. I left it behind to reunite with its home in the earth. Parting sweetly with somewhat regret we bid farewell a fortnight ago. The memories attached to its being ever present yet taking their place in my evolution. I have wondered while physical the meaning of existence only to be reminded between unitings of spirit and flesh. Now I see the value of existing physical, making choices for the spiritual growth while in a tangible form. The lessons derived on earth are always invaluable while once again setting on the horizon.

I can see for eons. My past, my present and future tumbling together in an energy vortex beyond physical understanding. Perhaps this is why the gift appears only between physical lives.

Each step I take resounds with beauty and deliverance. Each life I live brings my many selves closer to the energy of all existence. That energy has often been mistaken for god. Indeed while here on this horizon I can see the possibility of the confusion. Yet the simple understanding of such a complex equation always comes up the same. We are the energy and the energy is us. It is true I see it so clearly.

I will sit for a while here in the horizon. If you perchance come this way we could sit together for a while. The mingling of our essences would bring enlightenment to those not yet ready to see the whole horizon. If you cannot be here I will leave this note for you or someone to find. We move forward to our destiny.

Mathew.

Amos

Dear friend

I do not recognize my surroundings. There is a haze surrounding my perception. The origin unknown. I think yet I just float towards something I do not fully comprehend. Looking back over a phantom shoulder I see nothing useful in my quest. The motion of things about me causes lack of definition in the full picture of what I see. My experience in the flesh has distorted my focus. Originally this place was more clear. In retrospect I find that physical was indeed a unique experience. A joyride of sorts through one's emotional issues. The path so clear yet boggled by the thoughts of the flesh. Ordinary souls become god-like after a run in the cosmos as an incarnate.

I now perceive all of the lives I have participated in. The pattern jumping towards me abruptly. Surely the intent of my lives now a parade of my soul as it endeavors to evolve to the next level. We now understand the significance of it all. Each life an attempt to resolve issues presented by ourselves. I now am ready to move forward. I leave you with this. Drink in all your lives. Use the moments as an opportunity to evolve. Each breath a gift. Each deed a significant moment to who you are and who you are to become. Live it all fully. In the fullness become yourself and all the personalities you have cloaked yourself with. Understand there is a purpose to it all. When you are fully ready it all will become apparent.

Love + Light
Amos

Jack

Dear friend

The fire that burns inside has become a small ember barely visible. A rush of smoke escapes from me as I turn softly away from the flesh. Regrettably I linger a bit too long in this limbo of my life. I perceive that the transition should be swifter. Somehow melodious in its action. I retreat to old patterns in this moment by judging and scripting not only my life but my death. If I could force a laugh from this withered body I would. The last sustaining moments turn to my face and laugh back at me. A moment worthy of note should I survive this exercise.

In retrospect I admit being too serious for the good of my soul. A lighter, less arduous approach might have served me better. Instead I move forward in my way, stumbling often, tripping even more. I always wondered what this moment would be like. The fear always embraced me if I plunged too deeply into the thought. Attached so vigorously to my body and its personality, I felt so sure annihilation was the only possible outcome. So misguided was I. My whole perception of existence would have been altered had I known the truth. We are extended way beyond the physical. I inhale the last breath and exhale with my eyes open. Foolish am I to believe that physical eyes are the only thing that sees. Upon exhaling a glow surrounds me. Are my eyes opened or closed? I cannot tell. I look toward the light and feel humbled in the presence of something so powerful. Its beauty surpassing my wildest imagination. I seek guidance to identify this celestial presence. Who is it? Who is it. What is it?"

These questions so basic escape me and I feel lame in my questions. The presence envelops me and I realize that it is me. Or should I say all of me. I become one and feel at peace. The blending complete I do not even feel it necessary to get one last look at what is left behind. I carry all the essentials of that life. I move forward with my self. I find heaven is a reuniting of the whole. And the whole takes its place among the stars and is at peace. So am I.

Jack

Sebastian

Dear friend,

A lapse of time since I recognized my real self. So different from the images projected by my ego. A distortion occurred during this pattern that clouded my vision of my true path. It is odd how drama cuts the crooked edge on a tapestry so finely woven. In retrospect I see the damage done and seek to rectify it. Alas it seems that more physical living is involved in the process. I never cared for that type of existence. Now that I am here the clarity of my real views hit me abruptly. Thoughts are more fluid, desires more tangible. All the processes reacting immediately. No wait. I look about me and I see myself in various shades of evolution. In my mind's eye I perceived myself much further along. How astonishing to see the truth. My ego it seems has dominated my path every time. A moment to deal with it is received. My focus adjusted to see the levels of existence available.

The moments of eternity between lives are invaluable. How unfortunate most is lost upon re-entry. I sit and think about what I desire to achieve. I am shown many ways to trigger my memory at the precise moment of need.

I share these truths in hopes of helping others who do not remember. My agreement to help will allow my process to unfold in the next life. This letter is a trigger for some, a bit of fiction for others. The need is great and I fill the void. If only one is triggered to revelation all is well.

I Sign myself a soul traveler.

Sebastian

Stuart

Dear friend,

I have reached a milestone in my life. A moment really punctuated by diseased tissue and a lack of breath. Really a status not so envied by one's peers but inevitable all the same. The age of eighty is a minor milestone. One accomplished quite easily with proper maintenance and guidance of the body. The real accomplishment lies in the moments immediately following the last breath. A true test of character for those preoccupied with such things.

One would declare the preceding moments to be the most climatic. However I can attest that that is not quite true. Death at its best lasts mostly only a few seconds. The disablement is longer but the end is quite abrupt and usually painless. A mere wimp can survive a death. It is what follows that determines one's ability to be noted.

There is a precise knowing that makes an appearance upon the last exhale. A detailed journal of sorts of all transgressions and deeds. The ability to endure one's own actions tests the integrity and character of the individual. This reflection stares into the essence with open eyes. Survival depends on the ability of the essence to embrace its faults. This moment of personal forgiveness leads to an evolution of the Soul quite extraordinary. I am sure dear reader that in our physical state there came the assumption that we define survival in physical terms. We did not intend for you to believe the termination of the Soul clings to the moments "après morte". We are merely transcribing our experiences for your perusal.

All Souls experience death. It is an unconditional moment detailed by one yet "lived through by all". Prepare yourself for intense life scrutiny by yourself. You will be your worst critic and judge. You will decide the verdict. Embrace the journal and forgive yourself. In that moment you will enter heaven and become whole.

There is a slight nagging in the darkest corners of your being. It whispers of deceit and allows you to put aside this note. A look at oneself square in the face after the loss of the physical is devastating. This small voice beckons you to denial and your ultimate demise of the Soul. We beseech you to stand boldly. We have nothing to gain from this communication. It is a gift. Take it with you. Upon your last breath, remember this moment. It will be useful + comforting.

Stuart

315

Samba Serrado

Dear friend

"What do you bring with you?" the sphere of light inquired. In my confusion the answer escaped me entirely. I did not even have my physical form, so what could the question mean? In the preceding moments I had had quite a lot. So the question was misleading for I felt like someone who suddenly found themselves without their wallet. Grasping for any type of answer I replied "Nothing". A short reply but the only one that came to mind under this situation. I felt like a child in the midst of reprimand. The sphere of light seemed to melt into a human face. I suppose it was my own mind creating the form but it really looked like someone. I waited for a reply but none was forth coming. I do not recall how long I stood there or if I was really standing. All the physics I had studied were suddenly meaningless. There was not even recognition if there was an upright position.

So I will assume all is well. No focus on the laws of physics as I knew them. The light grows more defined and I swear the face appears amused. Is it me or my answer of nothing. "What have you brought with you?" The sounds reverberate and I still do not know. I had many things to bring however they are of no meaning now. This place does not sustain physical things. I search my memories and there is nothing. Again I am asked. Again I say nothing.

I feel sad. I feel that I could have brought something. Did I forget or did I just not see the importance. My mind a flurry of activity. I start to perceive the importance of bringing something with me. A lesson, a quote, a moment of love. These things can come with me. I now understand. Let me return and I will bring something. So I return to start over. With a new realization I evolve and I understand. I will write my thoughts on the next life pattern. Goodly I must be reborn. It is time.

Samba Serrado

Phyliss

Desperately

I inhale as deeply as I can

Desperately

I realize the moment of truth is near

Desperately

I think of any escape from the impending moment

Desperately

I claw at this body becoming so useless

Desperately

I look to anything to survive

Desperately

I run out of options

Desperately

I exhale the last breath

Desperately

I wait for annihilation

Desperately

I count seconds of time while

Desperately

I realize that time has ceased

Desperately

I now cling to my senses

Desperately

worried that I am about to cease to be

Desperately

My mind reels to anything that will sustain me

Desperately

the moments pass as my heart stops and my essence takes over

Desperately

I look for answers in the mist that surrounds me

Desperately

I turn to myself and observe an obsolete body

Desperately

I search for another vehicle only to be disappointed

Desperately

I search until I meet myself in the mist

Desperately

I recount my demise

Desperately

I search for a home to evolve to

Desperately

I see a passage to another life

Desperately

I avoid all revision in my attempt

to exist in a form that is familiar

Desperately

I move forward to that moment

319

Desperately

Not thinking that reflection may be of use

Desperately

I cry out to the cosmos in my new physical form

Desperately

beginning again without a pause to consider how

Desperately

I need to slow down to evolve into a new level of understanding of my self. My inner dynamics calling for a calming. My lack of heeding this call in my desperation has spiraled out of control. A level of understanding can only be achieved without desperation. There is no need. Calmly I attempt a new life in hopes of a new level. I am weary of all this desperation. I have circled this evolutionary spot for 279 lives.

Thank you for the opportunity to clarify the pattern. Your ability to blend with me has been beneficial. I now move forward. Thank you.

Phyliss

Umberto di Sanglia

Ashes. There is nothing left of who I was but ashes. My mortification of being annihilated rather fulfilled by this method of disposal. I am dead. Yet I still exist. Does this cancel my death? I am submerged in a pool of indecision and I grasp each moment with nonphysical hands. In my perception I exist as I was. A young man of twenty and then on the cusp of a fulfilled life. Yet this life so easily taken from me now a shadow of my thoughts. There are moments within myself where I mourn this tragic loss. A life plan gone awry by the random physical elements that fill each and every life.

Weary of the worry I rest what I consider my self. The thoughts of the final physical moments replay a thousand times. The "what ifs" protruding towards me in an eternal question.

This death process an enigma to all is an intimate bedfellow of mine. I have traced his profile many times. Now I embrace the end of this physical while contemplating my spiritual condition.

The realization of the importance but non-sustaining meaning of the physical grants me insight into what is truly my path.

The lives we are given are merely reflections of what our souls need to survive. Each drama a page in the story of us. The need for so many pages is confusing. One would think one life would be sufficient but it is not.

So now I leave you on my way to the next page of my personal evolution. My hope envelopes your recognition of what it truly is. Life is what you need to evolve. The serving size depends on you.

Go in peace.

Umberto di Sanglia

Tom

I quiver at the idea of returning to the physical. The input to those senses sends my spiritual pulse into a frenzy of beating. This far surpasses any expectation I may have.

If one measures time it has been many years since the last time I accumulated a sweat upon my brow. The act of physical labor so stimulating I could never forget it. My decision to return a great one. The choice a narrow margin of faith that requires a great jump for myself. I repeat another life pattern so that I may see for myself an evolution of my entire essence. Now in my more advanced state of evolution I am able to realize my potential and proceed with it in due course.

I share with those interested in my choices in securing a host for my education. Unlike those letters of leaving this is one of returning.

Contemplation of issues is not comfortable. Thus I speak quickly so that the process twirls about me and is finished before I blink an eye. Of course I do not have need of one yet.

The choosing is delicate. Proper thought is required in choosing. I review my patterns and my issues. Thus an appropriate list of potentials is presented. The choice not easy yet made in an obvious state of enlightenment. The state not easily kept requires immediate attention. There are 4 choices. The third one most viable for my evolution. I agree and the process begins. The most interesting moment bringing the entity into the form. It is more difficult then

325

leaving. Since the leaving requires expansion and the returning requires condensation.

I plunge into the abyss and I am again a physical being. There is joy yet a moment of sadness at the loss of contact so immediate to the spiritual. I feel a bit remorseful yet find my self looking forward to the evolution of my soul. This is only available through this process. So I proceed.

No illusions. No moments of euphoria. Just simple drama created to allow a glimmer of understanding to permeate my essence. I agree and it is good.

I breathe the air and become more.

Physical is a fine experience.

Tom

Stanley

Dear friend

Escape velocity pounds through me. A surge of energy similar to those of my youth spreads through my useless body. The surge rapidly propelling me into a personal orbit only surpassed by my first Ferris wheel ride. How long I have waited and dreaded this moment. I read all the books and prayed to the various gods of the moment. Mid life crisis thoughts hounding me at least a decade. Now that it is upon me I feel more alive than I have forever. My pulse quickens as my eyes widen to a new horizon. Quickly is this physical body forgotten. Only the memories attach themselves for the ride. Once I would have been anxious about a trip that did not include my body. Now it is simply a thought attached to essence that will carry itself with me to the new horizon.

I grieve but only for an instant. Whatever gives you power is what stays in the ride. My personal talent of art has manifested itself many times. Each time more evolved than the last. Curious how some things feel so familiar. I remember those feelings and at the time was not able to identify them. Now I see how various lives intersect and how all the experiences play upon each other. It is a rather delicate + complex game we play in the physical.

I am delighted with all the information. All of my questions answered silently by my life choices. Truly remarkable.

Now I step forward to the unknown. All is a blank tablet ready for me to script the next lesson.

I only hope that this knowledge stays with me or at least some of it. I bid whomever you are adieu. Perhaps we will meet again on another horizon.

Stanley

Benjamin Thomas 1778

Dear friend

As I slip into another place the realization of the force of the eternal now hits me full on. Never before does the magnitude of its force reveal itself so. All through this existence the now has been preached as a divine right given to all but controlled by none. A far off place seemingly with implications ever out of touch with who I thought I was. Now in these final moments I find myself digging my heels into the highway of eternity attempting to hold now in my feeble grasp. Never before has the importance engulfed me so. And never before have I realized its incredible force.

With all my might I throw myself in its path hoping to thwart its impending presence. It's all I've ever had but my attention often diverted elsewhere in my quest for spiritual enlightenment.

Thinking back on a life I proposed as well lived, I see the inconsistencies that have brought me to this particular spot. Perhaps less fixation on the past + future would have been more beneficial. Now in my twilight I experience that which is truly most important. Funny how clouded the image had been before. The clarity often an after thought no longer needed in the final moments.

In retrospect I find that more time devoted to the now would have proved more beneficial. I suppose hindsight is about as worthless as my gold watch on my path.

Just thought to share the experience. Perhaps there would have been a clear path if I had listened to one such as myself.

Thus the rantings of an old man echo off the walls of existence. The reverberation often just a melody to those still pursuing the now. Only one can hope that the focus keeps you forever in the moment. In the final moments it is all one wishes for. We accept our path. We have created it. It must be so.

Farewell

Benjamin Thomas 1778

The Creator of All

Dear friend

Forty days and a night I have spent locked in this room. Will no one let me escape unnoticed into the night? Who keeps me captive? I scream from my place. Truly this keeper is of the cruelest form. The walls have breath that inhales my thoughts and paints them vividly in an unending stream of insult. I have touched every nook searching for relief. Will no one help me? Long ago a being of sorts reached through the wall to touch me. Torture on its mind indeed. I was crafty though and dodged its hideous embrace. It spoke in soft whispers of paradise and such. Again I was too smart to fall for its lies. Did I tell you what it said? I can't remember if I did so I will repeat myself. It spoke of a person locked in his mind, thoughts taking shape with every thought he made. Ridiculous that someone would do such a thing to themselves. Isn't it? I know this being is most evil and has intentions of driving me mad. Let me out. Sprawling visions caress the walls again. A ghostly display of deep sadness. The being whispers again to my soul that I am the captor. Oh of course, I would lock myself in hell. The whisper continues with its lies. Forty days and a night I've spent in this room.

I give in to despair and pray for the end. The whispers continue until they implode inside my head. So cruel in their perseverance I begin to listen in hopes they will finally destroy me and give me some peace.

With resolution I rise to meet the embrace of this most cruel and hateful enemy. At last I will be destroyed and the torture will cease. As the being wraps itself around my down trodden essence there is a vibration. At last annihilation! I surrender. The dramas I witnessed and lived swirl before me in an explosion of thought. Suddenly the realization that the most cruel being...my captor, my torturer is...oh my God! it's me.

As the mist of my own negative creation dissipates I find the peace I so craved. In the arms of myself the creator of all.

[Note: This letter was not signed]

BaRTHOLOMEW

Dear friend

I cannot remember who I am. The air bitter sweet in my nostrils. If I exhale sharply a puff of smoke escapes my mouth. The area around me is foggy. One cannot see very far in any direction. I look down at my hands. There is a greyness about them and they are lined with protruding blue veins. It crosses my mind to wonder if the blood still flows through them. It is impossible to tell. I am on the outside looking in yet still looking out through eyes that can no longer see anything. Each moment fluid, passing through space like an aspiration. Am I a ghost? Is this the fate selected for those who cannot remember. To traverse through foggy space haunting the shell of former physical stages. Are those who stay blind to where they really are? Perhaps my fate will reveal itself. If not I am determined to move through the fog to any destination. I am curious if I will remember who I am. Will it really matter? I do know I am no longer physical. The path to this moment escapes me. Frustration occurs as I press myself to remember. Traces of past moments are passing before me. Not enough information to design an identity. The feelings leave me empty and doubtful of my future. Does a dead person really have a future? I cannot accurately describe my way of death. It all has evaporated from my mind.

The fog does not lift. It remains to torture me in my pursuit of myself. I start to walk hoping to find the edges of my confinement. I feel desperate for definition. A glimmer of hope precedes me and I chase after it arms wide open. The time in pursuit of my identity cannot be measured. Each movement non existent in this place of no time. It seems futile to pursue it farther. Perhaps there is no way to completely know who you are. Perhaps each identity is a mere fraction of the whole. And perhaps the separation from the whole invalidates the individual. I begin to feel that it does not completely matter who I last was. To look backward is unfulfilling. To look forward to the new identity and embrace it is perhaps the key to blending who you were with whom you are about to become. The edges of confinement fade considerably with each new thought. As I embrace my self and accept what cannot be changed I feel free. Free to become new. Free to be a part of all that is.

My search ends here. In the next life I have found out who I was. The knowledge comforts me and I begin again. This time with more clarity. The fog has lifted.

BaRTHOLOMEW

Selmia

Dear friend

The release of tension so immense was a miracle. Truly heaven in disguise. A moment of pure silence. A silence so void of the issues of physical life. That moment permanently imprinted upon me. Surely it is the heaven so written about by the gods.

I admit my fear of it. I admit my avoidance of it. My maniac quest to deceive and outwit it. However it is inevitable and we surrender reluctantly fearing that there will be no more moments. There will be no more us. Incredible now that that was even a thought or possibility.

A pristine moment held closely alters the essence for eternity. Such was this moment. My appreciation knows no limits. My next movement is unknown. I blend with all and become more. My destination not important for it implies a future. I live now in the moment only. I do not grieve for what is now returning to dust. I rejoice in the transition and hold dear the experiences of that form. It is a part of me and will continue to exist with me.

Unfortunate that death has been labeled so unfairly. It should not be a moment of fear. My culture implied an ending. A misunderstanding for it is truly a beginning. My words on paper rise from meaningless to important. Rejoice if you follow me. I cannot promise to wait but surely will leave my mark to encourage you. There are many more moments if you choose. Rejoice!

Selmia

Death Is Not What Has Been Told To Us

Dear friend,

Expanding my horizons has always been a desire of
mine. Each day of life an adventure. The daily routine
grind never really my best advocate. You can imagine
my delight when I arrived here. All that I ever desired
at my finger tips. A vast array of delicacies to be
savored. Death is not what has been told to us. Perhaps
in the beginning the stories were true but over the eons
they were distorted. My death was unplanned or should
I say unexpected. A freak accident. I abruptly found
myself in a small room. At first I thought I was
blacking out and that's how I got there. However now I
know that that small room was my perception. By
allowing my self to relax and respond to my death I was
able to make the small room larger until I had created
my own small universe. The physical body is merely a
shell. The important stuff is in your head. Thought is
the true life.

I realize I am being a bit vague but intricate detail is
still a challenge for me.

Just know that if you suddenly find your
circumstances to be in a small room do not despair.

You will be able to move forward out of it. We all do eventually but perhaps after this note you will be able to do so quicker.

We offer our guidance willingly.

Me.

Terrance B. Metla

Dear friend

Many times during a life path one finds himself on a plateau. There are no ups and downs merely a continuing pattern of whatever the essence has created. Often death is a vehicle for changing the energy associated with choices that enables one to escape the plateau. Thus I found myself one wintry eve some moments ago. The details of the physical mishap non memorable. However the process of spirit enabled my stagnant self to respond and move forward. Death is not necessarily a negative. It is often necessary to escape a monotonous condition created by the essence. So my dear friend do not mourn my death. It has been a release and a fulfillment that I have craved for so very long. My velocity towards the source of myself has increased 100 fold.

The transcending not possible before an ice storm now reeling towards the heavens. So sublime the feeling. So complete the thought. So enabling the separation from the flesh. We are one with the universe. And the universe is us. Gliding on a whisper of unidentifiable energy I reach to the center of my essence and feel my evolution to this new position. My association with God revealed in an implosion of energy. Truly magnificent. Truly the infinite manifestation of all my selves. The union of all us a mere thread in the tapestry of all existence.

Thus my interpretation of death now recorded for others. We are fulfilled.

Terrance B. Metla

[Dear friend

The after life so different than on would expect. The senses perceived manually in the physical are experienced psychically after death. The results are similar but eons apart. Thus the reason for physical and spiritual. Death is more traumatic for the living. This is something never occurring to myself before. There was always the mystery of the actual passing. Really no big event. One moment breathing air the next the nectar of the cosmos. Truly the later more fulfilling.

My first breath as a dead man came as a surprise. It was difficult to determine the actual moment. The soul protective allows only what the individual is ready for. Thus the difference in length of the process for each individual. Eternity is ever patient for those it loves. My experience like others fraught with disbelief and surprise. The adjustment quick but still a shock. The fear of individuality loss permeates the first few moments. Fear being negative draws illogical conclusions. As the fear subsides the blend with the other entity members is expanding rather than diminishing.

If there is anything to relate it is simply this. Death is not a period to a sentence. It is merely a pause and then a step to another evaluation of life. Nothing painful. Not fearful. Only the individual fear of change. To stay the same would be confining and not something to be pursued. The peeling of layers leads to the core. Each new layer a beginning. We suggest no fear. The process illuminates life. The boundaries of life should be limitless. The endless edges revealing all of who you really are. We will await you to assist.

Us]

Us

Dear friend

The after life so different than one would expect. The senses perceived manually in the physical are experienced psychically after death. The results are similar but eons apart. Thus the reason for physical and spiritual. Death is more traumatic for the living. This is something never occurring to myself before. There was always the mystery of the actual passing. Really no big event. One moment breathing air the next the nectar of the cosmos. Truly the later more fulfilling.

My first breath as a dead man come as as a surprise. It was difficult to determine the actual moment. The soul's protective allows only what the individual is ready for. Thus the difference in length of the process for each individual. Eternity to ever patient for those it loves. My experience like others fraught with disbelief and surprise. The adjustment quick but still a shock. The fear of individuality loss permeates the first few moments. Fear being negative draws illogical conclusions. As the fear subsides the blend with other entity members is expanding rather than diminishing

If there is anything to relate it is simply this. Death is not ~~about~~ a period to a sentence. It is merely a pause and then a step to another evolution of life. Nothing painful. Not fearful. Only the individual fear of change. To stay the same would be confining and not something to be pursued. The peeling of layers leads to the core. Each new layer a beginning. We suggest no fear. The process illuminates ~~this~~ life. The boundaries of life should be limitless. The endless edges revealing all of you ~~who~~ ~~to~~ really are. We will await you to assist

[Note: The few "cross outs" in this letter were done in real-time as the letter was being written. There was no editing done after the fact by the medium or anyone else.]

Ernest

Dear friend,

I view your existence from many angles. In the physical we were matched as lovers. The allure of lust overcame us as we plunged headfirst into our affair. That's all it was you know, at least for myself. Never did love or romantic thoughts enter my mind. I drank of the physical moment so enhanced by what I viewed as chemistry. So deeply entranced by the physical I had forgotten why I was there at all. Life was in the moment, flat, one dimensional. So get what you can while you can. A motto of sorts for me. I was most absorbed in my physique and the perfection of my features. I believed in God and thanked him but for all the wrong reasons. He was more of a fad than anything for me. I thought I had it all. Your body, a great career stunning looks, lots of money.

For all outward appearances a great life. I saw you but never really looked at you so out of touch was I.

My demise cam swiftly on a slippery road one October evening. You were not with me. I was party hopping looking for admiration of my perfect life. I remember the sound of a boom box or an extremely loud stereo. The other car was filled with young kids looking for a cheap thrill. They got a thrill in fact we all did but it wasn't cheap. The sound of grinding metal never seemed to end. My face became very warm and I felt something hit my head. Lights spun around me like a cheap disco from the seventies.

Then suddenly everything stopped. My first reaction was to jump out of the car to check for damage. Those idiot kids in the other car were going to be in a lot of trouble. My car was expensive.

There wasn't much left. I was furious. I turned to the other car and saw that it was on fire. Served them right, they should have been more careful. All four of them were standing together watching the car burn. In my anger I shouted at them for their stupidity. They had ruined my perfect car. How was I going to get home? They did not respond to me. They just stood there looking into the firs. Morons. I walked over to them to vent more of my frustration. As soon as I got close they looked at me in unison. Smiling they said, "He doesn't get it." I was about to lunge at them but they just melted away. Gone. Poof. Nowhere.

The car was in total flames but they were nowhere to be found. I then ran back to my car to get my cell phone to call the police. Then I saw it. A body humped over the steering wheel. The face was all mangled and there was a lot of blood. I pulled whoever it was back and then realized it was me.

I don't remember how long I stood there screaming. I don't remember what really happened next. All I do know is that an image of you came to me. You no longer appeared to me in the same way. There was a deeper feeling like I was seeing you for the first time.

I was seeing a lot of things for the first time too. My life was a series of physical fascinations. I had forgotten about the spiritual life the only one that really matters. So now I view you from a different angle. There is such beauty in your essence. My only hope is that we get the opportunity to try again in another physical life. This time I will be more aligned with the full dimensional life. Physical, Spiritual.

Remember me with love. It took my death for me to be alive again. And I will wait.

Love

Ernest

Dear friend,

I view your existance from many angles. In the physical we were matched as lovers. The allure of lust overcame us as we plunged headfirst into our affair. Thats all

...

life. Physical, Spiritual. Remember me with love. It took my death for me to be alive again. And I will exist.

Love
Ernest.

The last clear vision will physical eyes haunts my every move.
Twas not the essence of pearly gate or angels with golden halos.
Twas not St. Peter with the book of names allowed through
heavens gate. Twas not a meeting of those I knew who
awaited my arrival in paradise.

The last clear vision was none of these things and perchance
I could reveal many more. The picture of myself the one only I
knew gazing back into my fading vision. The one who lived
so many times and was bored to be doing it once more.
I thought I knew what I looked like. I thought I saw
very well. Seems though I was mistaken. There were many
layers linked to experiences by others who were part of me.
The knowledge withheld to be redeemed through
experience and remembrance. Too bad the information
did not translate. Too bad it would have to wait again
till next time.

The last vision of myself haunts me so. I was so much
more than I thought. My life more meaningful to the
whole than I dared realize. My ordinary life an
intricate part to the whole scheme of things. Too bad
I did not realize my worth. Too bad my last vision
was that of a stranger.

My wish for you fair reader: Look at yourself
before you cross over. Gaze deeper into your eyes, they
are truly the windows. I await another round
perhaps we will start together. Remember who you are.
Look deeper. Remember.

   Elizabeth

Elizabeth

The last clear vision with physical eyes haunts my every move. T'was not the essence of pearly gates or angels with golden halos. T'was not St. Peter with the book of names allowed through heaven's gate. T'was not a meeting of those I knew who awaited my arrival in paradise.

The last clear vision was none of these things and perchance I could reveal many more. The picture of myself the one only I knew gazing back into my fading vision. The one who lived so many times and was bored to be doing it once more. I though I knew what I looked like. I though I knew very well. Seems though I was mistaken. There were many layers linked to experiences by others who were part of me. The knowledge withheld to be redeemed through experience and remembrance. Too bad the information did not translate. Too bad it would have to wait again till next time.

The last vision of myself haunts me so. I was so much more than I thought. My life more meaningful to the whole than I dared realize. My ordinary life an intricate part to the whole scheme of things. Too bad I

354

did not realize my worth. Too bad my last vision was that of a stranger.

My wish for you fair reader. Look at yourself before the cross over. Gaze deeper into your eyes, they are truly the windows. I await another round perhaps we will start together. Remember who you are. Look deeper. Remember.

Elizabeth

Andrew

Dear friend

I never learned to read. The one regret in a somewhat happy life. Of all the opportunities presented it was the one I never experienced.

I suppose you wonder how I am now able to write this note. Actually I am merely thinking my thoughts out loud and they are translated to the page. A real modern gizmo at that. A right easy way to talk to you. Never did this moment cross my mind when I was living. I was very caught up with just eating to tell the truth. It was the one focus of living. So much that I did not have the time to dwell on much else.

I was born 1829 AD in Harrisburg Pennsylvania. My father a dairy farmer. We as a family made smoked cheese and of course provided milk to our local market. It was all I knew.

My older brother Jacob raised me. My parents caught in a grinding motion of survival that they never escaped. I never thought of God. He was someone who lived in the corner church who only appeared on Sundays. Somehow he was never around when we were extremely hungry.

I caught my hand in a grist mill when I was 11 years old. It hurt so bad I nearly fainted. Jacob got me out but the bone was shattered. I never regained use of the hand. It hung at my side as a constant reminder of my now helpless existence. I learned to be productive with my left hand. "There is no room on a farm for free loadin", as my father would say. I never understood why that happened. Many looked at it as a mark of the devil. A repentance for evil thoughts and misdeeds. I was a boy of eleven, what evil could have lurked there.

I spent 10 years trying to survive, trying to eat and live. I was not unhappy merely driven to sustain the physical form. In retrospect I understand. I was very young at the process.

I fell off a wagon on the way to market when I was 17. My head hit a rock and I remained asleep. My family mistook my dilemma and buried me. I suffocated and died. Perhaps I should be resentful. Perhaps not. I now see so much that to return to that place would be futile. It was a step in my evolution. I now await another host. This time I think reading will be a priority. That particular life provided me with a reference point. I now know that I am a young soul on a path to knowledge. No life is useless. Oh by the way the event with my hand was a symbol of my inability to reach out for more in that life. Now I know to desire more. Pretty ordinary but certainly important in the next step. I want to learn to read.

Andrew

Dear friend
I never learned to read. The one regret in a somewhat happy life. Of all the opprotunities presented it was the one I never experienced.

...

for more in that life. Now I know to desire more. Pretty ordinary but certainly important in the next step. I want to learn to read.

Andrew

Part III

APRIL CRAWFORD

Some Quotes from *"Parting Notes"*

"You do not know us by name. We exist in the peripheral of physical life. The opportunity afforded to us...was indeed a precious gift. There are many levels of living...All the levels are accessible but communication between them not always available. Souls traveling together sometimes get separated. Without...assistance messages of encouragement solace and love cannot jump the barrier...You are about to be enlightened. All of us anticipated your arrival. Read these gifts...We are all alive and well. We only wish to share the marvel of all existence. Each of these letters will alter one person's life, or perhaps many in unison. After you have read them, share them. That was the intent in which they were written.

Read with love.
All of us."

"The thoughts of a dead man are valuable. The creation of a map to the hereafter is now available...You too shall prevail in the hereafter. The body will turn to dust but it is only a costume for the

361

real you. That which you perceive as you inside your head will remain. It is true. I am proof."

From: Thomas Johnson

"However this is my note to you. I choose to tell you that it is nothing. A stroke of midnight, a whisper of wind through the trees. No matter what pain the physical present presents the end result is serene and beautiful. It has never been otherwise for me."

From: Theodore

"There is a level of existence that encompasses more than you can comprehend. Now that I have left my physical form I can embrace that existence and become one with it. In the physical we are preoccupied with physical needs. Sometimes those needs help us evolve other times they serve as a distraction. I now see the whole picture. We communicate to open your eyes. Spiritually or physically to another way of living. And we desire to comfort any fears that you associate with the end of physical existence. It simply does not apply to the vastness of your soul. Our goal is to communicate this. There is no other purpose.

No drama exists here. It is petty and unworthy of the richness of this plane. Close your eyes and visualize if you desire a place beyond any expectation. If you can create it in your mind multiply it by a thousand fold. That is where you will be when the physical is shed and you become your true self."

From: T.

"Death is not what you suppose. It's not an ascension to the light, it's not an ending to a drama. There are many things it is not and I could go to eternity with them. I'll tell you what it is though. It is a major line crossing that should not be feared. The fear can be eliminated by beginning to cross minor lines placed by you & others in your earth plane existence on a daily basis."

From: AmbrosE

"I made a mental note to put in a complaint about the aloofness of the hospital staff. Everyone just looked through me. Here I am a very sick woman out of bed for the first time in months and no one seemed to care.

I plodded back to my room very pissed indeed, the door swinging easily and I was stunned at the picture before me. There I was still in bed eyes closed asleep. I could hear a clock ticking from off in the distance. Counting off time which of course now was irrelevant to me.

Suddenly I got it. A new sense of reality descended upon me and I was transformed. I am now on a new journey to a new place. I just wanted to let some one know. There's so much more."

From: Adrienne

"Physical pain is but a dim memory to me now. Yes in those last moments it was difficult but the pain was meant to give us clarity. I know it sounds strange but in my position the clarity survives and is useful.

I rejoice at the opportunity to tell you. I am fine. Different but more than whole as we knew it. Live your life with this positive lesson. I will wait for you. The window is closing..."

From: Daphne

"DEATH IS LIKE JUMPING ON THE TRAMPOLINE. I KNOW. I HAVE ALREADY MADE THE LEAP. I WILL NOT ABANDON YOU NOW. TAKE MY HAND WHEN YOU ARE READY AND WE WILL JUMP TOGETHER.

YOUR BIG BROTHER,

ME."

From: YOUR BIG BROTHER

"When I first realized my death I was out in the garden. Of course nothing I ever planted grew properly...On this particular morning however I noticed that the tomatoes were rather red & luscious...I reached down to pick one. It was immediately replaced by another. I knew something was up.

...Now I was sure I was dead or something.

...In each life we create that which is perfect for our growth. It may not always make sense but you have to look at the big picture."

From: Focus

"Fear should have enveloped me when they caught me, however defeat can be a powerful drug. Giving up seemed like the only alternative. Closing my eyes I can remember the sound only. I deserved to die. I was a thief and they were the robbers. Pretty much the same thing if you think about it. We were all the bad guys. It never occurred to me that I would end my life as I live it. Violently.

Now that I can see it with more clarity, I realize that life and your actions in it are a careful balance. In my haste to have it all I missed some important issues.

...Of course now I get it after I find my self bleeding & dead on the floor of my mama's shed."

From: Giving

"When the end came it was so abrupt that it knocked me off my feet. There was no pain. No warning, no time. There were moments of reenactment. Stuff I remember happening but had forgotten all the minute details. Now they came forward like a fresh line of ideas...

There were many plans made for the life I lived while knowing you. I was great at the future but lousy in the present. By betting on what I would do in the future I thought I was buying time. There was the error. The future I was planning for, the me I was going to be never existed. They were cut off when the blood clot hit my brain. Gone. Dead. Done.

You see by viewing my life from the future I enabled my self to be satisfied with where & what I was. Not that there was anything drastically wrong with me. You know I was a pretty good guy. I just had a wrong angle on my view.

Physical life is but a glimmer in what I know now. It is precious and it is immediate. Do not delay anything of importance until tomorrow. That is the lesson. Of course there are many lessons to learn & physical existences to live. We thought only to tell you since this writing opportunity presented its self to us in our now. We thank the channel. And we thank you my friend for reading."

From: Opportunity Exists in the Now

"As my vision clouded I saw those beautiful eyes of yours begin to tremble from within. My last thought was the realization that you would blame yourself. But then of course it was too late.

So now I write to you from another place. I have tamed the fears that distorted my path in the life I shared with you. My friends here have helped me regain my worth. I am whole. And this opportunity to write to you has been a blessing. Please take my love with you from this life to the next. Do not blame yourself for my fears. They had nothing to do with you. Look fear in the eye with boldness. Do not let it chase you into a dark corner. Instead remember my love.

We will have more sunny days.

Me (Mom)"

From: Do Not Let Fear Chase You

"There is so much to tell and such a small window of opportunity. There is a vast space waiting for each person. Waiting to be molded into something of your choosing...Take comfort in the knowledge I am creating and expanding my universe in hopes that when you are finally "here" I will be the one to guide you. The window closes now but be assured we await another opportunity.

Remember this."

From: TESSiE

"You see I lived a rather ordinary life. Nothing profound occurred that would give the appearance of anything important. I was born. I lived. I survived. I raised a family. What could I tell you of my death? Nothing spectacular. A cancer began to deteriorate my colon and that was it. I can remember turning my head to speak to my wife Sylvia but I simply could not move my lips any longer. I would have liked to tell her not to cry but I couldn't. It surprised me to be so lucid but not to be able to let anyone know I was allright.

I watched with fascination my funeral and ceremony. My body now was detached from what was really me. Not important, although I really thought my blue eyes were great. Silly thoughts but you do think of those things. I was greeted by an entourage of beings none of whom I recognized. My form or what I presumed to be me was changing rapidly. Oh not deterioration by any means. It was changing from identity to identity. I was told we all keep the experiences from all of our lives tucked away in our essence. Now that that essence was free of physical bonds those lives came to the forefront. It was unbelievable. I was asked what I had learned and what did I teach while physical."

From: "Take A Moment To Believe In Something Fantastic"

"The accident or should I say my predetermined physical end did not allow me to be able to render a few last pieces of advice. I also know how much this disturbed you. So with that let me continue.

...Do not let my death stifle your joy. Know that I have not ended merely evolved. I did not suffer physically and now that I have been able to communicate with you my heart suffers no longer. Keep the words of this note next to your heart. Whether you believe they are from me or not does not matter. The essence of my connection with you will become enhanced by reading this. Be joyful. We will meet again although perhaps in different circumstances. Go now and be wonderful. I am content. So should you be.

I love you."

From: "I am Writing To You As a Gift"

"Through the physical manifestation of this letter I have achieved the ultimate focus. To blend through a physical form not my own requires great concentration. I have attempted this process many times without success. They have told me here that this achievement allows for many "good" events to unfold. I am honored to participate and I offer thanks for the opportunity to 'focus'".

From: "Better Choices"

"Nonetheless I remember inhaling, looking into the eyes of all those I loved. Upon exhaling all of the faces blended into ones that I still knew but were different. I realized that these "new" faces were those of ones I had known before. There was not a blinding light nor a tunnel merely a change of scenery. I can remember wondering when I would finally be dead. I looked around at the faces before me and asked. I was told that the transition had occurred and I was now "alive" not dead. They likened it to a snake shedding its skin, merely a "wrap" that no longer was of use. I turned around hoping for a glimpse of my former self but it was gone. Only existing now in my memory.

Expecting to feel remorse I was surprised when the only feeling I had was joy. There was no pain and all my parts seemed to be in working order. My friends greeted me with a warmth forgotten in the bonds of physical. I was home."

From: "What It's Like to Die"

"Physical death is the beginning. The beginning of the cycle created to allow one to evolve and grow in the chain of evolution. This process brings us closer to the source of all life...I implore you to consider the possibility that I am correct. Try for a moment to accept death as the beginning. Fear it not...Your acceptance is not obligatory. My wish for communication is fulfilled."

From: "Physical Death Is The Beginning"

"Let's just say that death was a friend that eased the suffering in my soul. I thought it would be the end. Oh was I mistaken...

...I was standing on a bridge in Vermont. It was a quaint area and instead of enjoying the surroundings I was again brooding about some delusional mishap in my life. I thought that by jumping off the bridge a page would be turned closer to my annihilation. After declaring my intentions I calmed down and decided to wait for another time. Besides I had gotten a lot of attention from my companion that filled me up somehow. Suddenly death lost its appeal. I stepped down from the bridge only to move directly into the path of a drunken driver. He was doing 90 miles an hour.

The impact sent my body sailing into the air. I was conscious but it all seemed like a movie clip in slow motion. My hip hurt a lot and I was wondering how it would feel when I hit the ground. The sky looked ever so blue and my nose felt like it was getting a burn from the sun. Did I wear sunscreen? I had an eternity to ponder over it before I hit. I do not remember if it hurt.

I woke up in a hammock in my mother's back yard. It was still sunny. The screen door slammed and I turned to see my mother bringing out a tray of lemonade. This provoked an avalanche of memory which led me to the realization that my mother had been dead for 10 years. My mom brushed my brow in a familiar loving way that proved to me that it was actually her. Returning her touch it dawned on me that if she were really in front of me then I too was dead. The thought was alarming."

From: "Oh Was I Mistaken"

"I write this letter from another place in hopes that there may be another with the same questions as I. Perhaps this letter will answer some long awaited question by someone who needs to know what does it feel like to die?

There is no need to fear. I was "killed in an accident caused by a diesel truck. The car I was driving was hit almost head on when it jumped a center meridian on the freeway...It was so quick that I barely had time to panic...Death did not occur to me! After a few moments I opened my eyes. Everything around me was in chaos but I felt strangely calm...There was fear that the truck would explode and there were 2 guys trying to pull a man from a smoldering piece of metal...

...Pounding on the window it was determined that the guy inside was most likely dead...Puzzled I moved forward and easily slipped inside the wreckage...The adrenaline feeling came again when I pulled him back to reveal his face. It was me...

I started to laugh. It was a deep belly laugh that I had not experienced for many years. I was dead! I had died in a horrible accident and it was over. There was nothing to fear. Only my own self imposed thoughts.

So you see, death will come but not annihilation. What ever the experience is there will be a moment for you to look back on it like any other experience you've had. If I had known this it would have impacted my life. Thus the reason for this letter. Hopefully it will impact you in some positive way."

From: "I Write This Letter From Another Place"

"MY MESSAGE, SO SIMPLE. 'I AM HERE'. I OCCUPY THE SAME SPACE ONLY WITH LESS DENSITY. AS YOU WILL."

From: Daniel

"You see death is as easy as you want to be. The same principle of though creating reality exists here also…
Do not allow fear of nothingness to hold you. For if you do that is exactly what you will have after death…nothing.
You can begin anytime to formulate that which you would like to have. It's all there in you. And you can create anything you want.
Yes that is what I had to tell you. I must return now to my after life. There is much to do."

From: "I've Something to Tell You"

"Your soul has asked why…and we have answered. It is not the end of our partnership. There will be another time. Know this."

From: "Dear Mother"

"We have nothing to gain from this communication. It is a gift. Take it with you. Upon your last breath, remember this moment. It will be useful + comforting."

From: Stuart

"I write with awe and genuine surprise. Spending this last existence totally convinced there was not a divine afterlife. I now rescind those thoughts.

…My best friend Chad sat with me…I closed my eyes becoming lulled by the tone of his voice. I don't remember when it changed but suddenly it wasn't Chad anymore. There was someone new beside me…

I opened my eyes. There was a moment of blurryness then I focused on the most beautiful blue eyes I had ever seen...

My vigilant friend came to my side and stood with me. It dawned on me who it was. My shock made me unable to speak for many moments. This person was angelic. I was dead, yet I still was. My eyes filled with tears at my lack of belief. I had been so mistaken...No matter what you think there is more. The only one fooled is yourself if you believe there is nothing more. It is the one belief that will not come true."

From: "I was Dead, Yet I Still Was"

"All of us here do not regret dying. It is an evolutionary process. One does live forever...

Fear not death. It is not an ending. Just a transition."

From: "All of Us Here Do Not Regret Dying"

"One fellow did show up though. A plain little man that I had seen many times in my life...He asked in the softest of voice if I were ready...

Smiling he told me that I should come with him. Didn't he realize I was waiting to die? The face that reflected me spoke again with this line. 'You have'.

I can tell you now that death is smooth. You may wait for it, defy it, run from it, or face it with your eyes open. It comes silently and the result is wondrous."

From: "I Can Tell You That Death Is Smooth"

"My message is simple. 'You live on.' In an altered state but alive. I know that it would have been important for me to know that when I was alive in the physical. I hope it gives you comfort. Without a physical body it is different. One learns to create what one needs. Perhaps creation is a process to be practiced. Just know that all is well. Go in peace and love."

From: Rachel

"As you exhale the exuberance of life envelops you. It is the same in death, only this time the exhilaration is not fleeting. It builds.

We speak so that you can remove the shadow of fear. We speak to lead you to forever. We also speak for those who cannot or will not. We appreciate the opportunity. That being a gift itself.

Your experience will be enhanced without the fear. There are others with different stories. We hope you resonate with one."

From: Amelia

"I don't know when the exact moment of death came. I didn't feel pain. I had not taken a breath for quite a while. There was a prickly feeling in my hands. I was paralyzed but fully conscious. My whole life began to come alive before me. I saw it all. I began to wonder how long I could stand there while I was dead. I knew it, it just didn't happen like I thought it would. My body was not functioning but I was alive. My whole belief in life was turned around in that brief eternal moment.

I have been dead for nearly a year now. There have been indications that I should move forward and learn more about my surroundings. I cannot however leave you until you hear me. This letter is my last resort. I am trapped in your sorrow. It is my hope you will read this and be assured I am allright."

From: Henry 1987

"My only opportunity has presented itself in the person who writes for those who cannot."

From Jeffrey

"SUDDENLY I KNEW I WOULD NOT INHALE AGAIN. AND YOU KNOW NOTHING CHANGED. THE ROOM REMAINED. I SUDDENLY FELT LIKE AN ICE CREAM CONE. I GOT UP OUT OF BED AND WENT TO THE KITCHEN. I HAD NOT BEEN UP IN QUITE A WHILE. AS I REACHED IN THE FREEZER I REALIZED THAT THIS WAS THE MOMENT I HAD DREADED MY WHOLE LIFE. AND HERE I WAS EATING ICE CREAM.

I WANTED TO LAUGH. THEN I WANTED TO CRY. I SETTLED ON FINISHING THE ICE CREAM."

From: Raymond

"You wonder why we write? We do for the reassurance to you that there is more. It is not like anything you could imagine right now. You will remember when you open your spiritual eyes. There will be rejoicing. Do not fear death. That is our message to you."

From: T Mary

"I felt a hand on my shoulder but I was afraid to look up. There was a gentle voice that sounded familiar. I was told that I could control what was happening. Thought creates reality and I was running rampant through the process. All I had to do was slow down. Think slowly. I could be anywhere I wanted from now on. The truth of it was that I was dead.

Funny. I wasn't upset. I opened my eyes and looked immediately into my brother's eyes. I had not seen them for so very long."

From: Arthur

"It is the noble thing to do. My continued existence serves as a beacon of hope to all those fearful of annihilation through death. It simply is not so. I am proof. You may disregard me. Indeed I hope not. I cannot offer validity other than my own testament. I watched my funeral. I felt the life force leave my body and continued. I was the life force not my physical form.

When your moment arrives perhaps you will remember this letter. Perhaps it will ease your anxiety. Perhaps I will be there to meet you. Perhaps we will connect and be friends. It is my hope."

From: Anton

"I wanted to feel the grass press against my back. All these things I did feel when I ran from you that morning. In complete abandon without any caution I stepped in front of that bicycle. It shouldn't have killed me but my skull had not completely developed and the damage was severe. It was a moment however of complete joy for me. I was able to consume the whole experience in an instant. My only regret is your sadness. Please do not feel badly. The experience was in line with my growth. Know that by my lack of perception I was killed, not by anything you did or didn't do.

Know that I still exist and that you will experience my essence again. Perhaps in a different format. I understand your isolation but you are choosing to put yourself there. This experience has benefited us both. I can't say I'll wait for you but know that our essences are drawn to each other. The magnetism will occur again.

Be at peace. Know no guilt. It was my choice. Stand up and live this life you have taken. It's the only way to reunion."

From: Sebastian

"I bid whoever you are a great forever."

From: SABAN

"The need is great and I fill the void. If only one is triggered to revelation all is well.

I Sign myself a soul traveler."

From: Sebastian

"My ability to create was beyond my expectations. This place, my universe was more beautiful than anything I had ever experienced. Truly a new lease on life. Different but equally exciting. And most importantly eternal. To be able to be here I had to shed the physical. It was nothing compared to this. Death is necessary for spiritual evolvement. We do not need our bodies to exist. Death is a timely process by which we realize our full potential. It is only dark + silent until we offer our souls and surrender. I no longer feel regret. Only appreciation of the process. I know that there are those who cling to physical even more

385

vehemently than I. This is the reason for my communication, to tell you it's okay to let go.

What awaits you is spectacular if you only let it be so."

From: Mathilde

"Death should not be described as an ending. It's thought provoking but so untrue. It is merely an adapting to a new set of surroundings. My only desire in this communication is to share my awareness of what a simple process it is."

From: Seemo

"Attempt to connect with the energy of life. Give of yourself to the comfort of others. Through this you will be able to find me. I exist through divine energy now. I continue to evolve. My heart is filled with love for you."

From: Hector: "We Are But A Breath Apart"

"Then I saw it. A body humped over the steering wheel. The face was all mangled and there was a lot of blood. I pulled whoever it was back and then realized it was me."

From: Ernest

"If there is anything to relate it is simply this. Death is not a period to a sentence. It is merely a pause and then a step to another evaluation of life. Nothing painful. Not fearful. Only the individual fear of change."

From: Us

"My wish for you fair reader. Look at yourself before the cross over. Gaze deeper into your eyes, they are truly the windows."

From: Elizabeth

"I fell off a wagon on the way to market when I was 17. My head hit a rock and I remained asleep. My family mistook my dilemma and buried me. I suffocated and died. Perhaps I should be resentful. Perhaps not. I now see so much that to return to that place would be futile. It was a step in my evolution. I now await another host."-

From: Andrew

Acknowledgements And Thanks

There are a number of people who share their talents and abilities with humanity in order to further awareness of the afterlife and in the process help people to enhance their daily physical lives and reduce society's fear of death. We wish to acknowledge and thank all of them and in particular the following individuals:

John Edward, Rosemary Altea, George Anderson, Dannion Brinkley, James Van Praagh, Jane Roberts, Robert Butts, and Chelsea Quinn Yarbro.

To all of those on the other side who have chosen to talk with us, answer our questions, and have fun with us on so many occasions, in particular

VERONICA

T

Gabriel

Madeline

Lizette

Ish

Osco

Titus

Olaf

and all of the rest including all those who wrote a parting note,

THANK YOU!

About the Author

April Crawford first discovered her psychic abilities spontaneously and dramatically in 1989 while dining with friends. She has had the ability to allow individuals on the Other Side to converse through her ever since. *"Parting Notes"*: A Connection With The Afterlife came about at the request of those on the Other Side. April and those on the Other Side who speak via her mediumship have given both private and group consultations over the past 10+ years to friends and small intimate groups but her abilities as a deep trance psychic voice medium have until now been largely kept as a closely guarded secret. This is April's first book. April lives with her husband Allen, her beloved Chow Chows, cats, and many other pets in Los Angeles, California.

Printed in the United States
89180LV00004B/60/A